To
Alexandre, Noemi, Ricardo and Leonardo Kaplan

The Jews Were Internauts

Archaic Accesses to the Internet

Nilton Bonder

Order this book online at www.trafford.com
or email orders@trafford.com

Most Trafford titles are also available at major online book retailers.

Printed in the United States of America.

ISBN: 978-1-4269-3570-1 (sc)
ISBN: 978-1-4269-3571-8 (hc)
ISBN: 978-1-4269-3572-5 (e-b)

Library of Congress Control Number: 2010908700

*Our mission is to efficiently provide the world's finest, most comprehensive book publishing
service, enabling every author to experience success. To find out how to publish your book, your
way, and have it available worldwide, visit us online at www.trafford.com*

Trafford rev. 07/16/2010

www.trafford.com

North America & international
toll-free: 1 888 232 4444 (USA & Canada)
phone: 250 383 6864 • fax: 812 355 4082

THE JEWS WERE INTERNAUTS

Ancient Access to the Web

The rebbe of Saragossa said:
"We can always learn something about everything that exists in
this world!
--What can we learn about a train, for example?
a disciple challenged him.
--That because of a second, we can lose everything.
--And a telegraph?
--That every word is counted and
we will be charged for it.
--And the telephone?
-- That what we say here is heard there."

-- And the internet? ....

*For this commandment, which I command thee this day, it is not
hidden from thee, neither is it far off. It is not in heaven, that thou
shouldest say, Who shall go up for us to heaven, and bring it unto us,
that we may hear it, and do it? Neither is it beyond the sea, that thou
shouldest say, Who shall go over the sea for us, and bring it unto us,
that we may hear it, and do it? But the word is very nigh unto thee,
in thy mouth, and in thy heart, that thou mayest do it.*

Deut. XXX:11-14

TABLE OF CONTENTS

THE LAST FRONTIER OF VIRTUALITY

PART I

WINDOWS

PROPHECIES ABOUT THE INTERNET

Just fewer than three millennia ago, Biblical prophets began a strange process. Although they originated in the ancient schools of seers, and bore the title of *chazon*, seer, or the vision, associated with this practice, the Biblical prophets clearly represented a new trend.

Unlike their ancestors, they were not prophets working diligently in the dimension of time. They worked in the dimension of space, of place. The Biblical prophets tried to see what others didn't see, not necessarily in time, but in place. Their prophecies are not about what will come to pass, though they have often been understood as such, but about what was happening in the present.

They did not foresee the future, but looked into the present with such transparency that they could warn their people about the future contained in that present. The Biblical prophets had their eyes open not to an overlaying of eras, but an overlaying of places. They discovered "windows" that didn't serve to check on future eras, but on the many places contained in what appears to us as only one place. They were wracked and terrified not by the future that could be seen, nor by the spirits who knew what was to come, but by this strange entity that spoke to them of any place, and made them see their place with different eyes. What was shown to them were not events to come, but a different place that existed in the very same place that others could not perceive.

Their words were configured in ethics because they tried vehemently to explain to those who could not see this other place, a larger landscape than the horizon they could grasp.

"Don't you see?" asks the prophet. Here, in this place, there is something just as hidden in the dimension of space as what we imagine to be hidden by the future. Place, the medium of existence, has as much or more to teach us about the meaning of existence, than what will be. For the first time, human beings woke up to the question, "Where are we and where might we be?", instead of "Where did we come from and where are we going to?"

This questioning no longer arises as a discourse on history, but a discourse on ethics; not about what will be in time, but what can be seen here of that which is beyond this place. This new kind of seer saw in place what others did not, and unlike those who said they saw the future (something that for some reason seemed plausible to most people), he was misunderstood, and called *meshugah*, crazy.

The purpose of this book is to reflect on past knowledge of the concept of place, making use of the Internet, a fascinating instrument and metaphor. It will also, as it must, speculate about future knowledge of place. Its structure is archaic, and it is no doubt prisoner of the paradigm deriving from time, not place.

For that reason this book may at times seem more the task of a seer than of a Biblical prophet. But it will be easier to visualize what we cannot see, describing it with structures that we can. And even though it might not free itself from being about time, about the past and the future, it aims to spark the feel of something that one day will be better understood without relying on the metaphor of history. This book may then become as obsolete as the 3D glasses used to watch movies in the 1950s; a book from a Flintstones world where all is possible, if made from stone, only because we do not know how to use other materials.

Science fiction, if we can call it that way, was for the prophets not so much the obsession of finding out that which the future was to unveil but space. They dreamed not of traveling in time, neither did they dream of traveling on space, but within space. For that they needed windows and portals.

CONCEPT OF ACCESS

Actually, what was offered to the Biblical prophets was not the chance to leave a place, nor even to travel through time; what was made possible for him was access.

Enriched by its use in cybernetics, access has become a keyword for understanding the true nature of media (means). Media (means) permit access to something which really exists, but that prior to access, could not be reached or perceived. Among past representations of access, the idea of place appears to hold great importance. In two ways, the Biblical text associates "place" and "access": 1) every place is an access and 2) any place is an access.

Every place is an access:

For those who have "access" to the Hebrew language, I recommend taking the time to look at your Bible, to accompany the original text and benefit from its clarity. We will look at Genesis 28:10. The text describes the episode in which Jacob flees home, fearing his brother will kill him.

We are told of Jacob's journey from Beer-Sheva to Haran, from one place to another. He then "lighted upon a certain place, and tarried there all night, for the sun was set." The Hebrew construction is quite unusual- *va ifgah ba-makom*- he was caught, stained or touched by the place. The text does not say *be-makom*, in a place, but *ba-makom*, in the place. What place? Neither the text nor the context say.

On that place he spent his first night after leaving home. The text is very concrete about the hardness of that moment: "Now he took one of the stones of the place and set it at his head and lay down in that place." It is as if the text is trying to address explicitly the notion of place. We are no longer in or at a place, or at the place, but "in this place", *ba makom ha-hu*. In this place Jacob has his famous dream where he sees a ladder with angels going up and down. When Jacob awakes, we read (28:16): "Certainly there is G-d in this place, and I did not penetrate* it!" He feared and said, "How dreadful is this place! This is none other but the house of G-d, and this is the gate of heaven!" This place, every place, is *shaar*, an opening, an access, to the heavens.

Touched by the intensity of this moment in his life, by his awe and pain, Jacob gains access to another understanding of the place where he is. This place, where he truly meets himself, is not limited to physical place (where he is situated); there is in it access to another place where he truly was, without realizing it.

Any place is an access:

In another passage of Genesis (21:17), the text tells of the expulsion of Hagar, Abraham's wife, together with their son Ishmael. In the middle of the desert without water, on the brink of despair, Hagar tried to leave the child, to avoid seeing his death. At that instant, G-d heard the child's cry and said, "What aileth thee, Hagar? Fear not; for G-d hath heard the voice of the lad where he is (*Ba-asher hu-sham*)!"

To better understand this passage, Reb Nachman of Bratslav* brings up another verse (Deut., 4:29): "From thence thou shalt seek the Eternal thy G-d." Reb Nachman then asks, "From thence, where? He answers -- from the very place in which he finds himself (*ba-asher hu sham*)."

---

* Chassidic spiritual leader who lived in the 19th century.

Any place allows access.

It is interesting to note that in the text preceding Jacob's dream, the fundamental word is *makom*, place. In the Deuteronomy text, it is as if this word were being avoided, using "thence" instead. The literal translation of *ba-asher hu sham* is "in which he is there". The designation of place comes from the word sham, there. Just as Jacob's text emphasizes "here" (*makom ha-ze*, this place), Ishmael's text emphasizes "there". This is because access exists just as much here as there. In other words, here and there can be the same place, as long as the correct access exists. Any place can be every place, and every place can be any place.

JUMPING THE PATH

This strange idea that makes Jacob shake, that this place is the place-- any or every place-- depends on the password he uses: *shaar*, or portal of access. Countless times in the literature of the Kabbalah*, we find the idea of *k'fitsat ha-derech*, which means literally, jumping the path. The Kabbalah masters believed it possible to jump from one place to another apparently distant location, without passing through an intermediate point. This was a kind of teleporting or magic that could be utilized as long as the master knew a *shaar*, a portal of access.

The secret actually lies with Jacob's discovery. The ability to gradually transform a place into the place, and then, this place, is the portal for jumping the path. And this is what we do today, precariously, with our means/computers. From one place (a microcomputer), we access a place (a network), which isn't any place at all, and we turn another place into the place where we are. With the means we have created, we are just beginning to find out about the art of jumping the path and perceiving the portals in space that lead to other spaces. The means we produce with scientific **knowledge** are models of structures similar to those found in the world around us. They can revolutionize the way we think about being.

More than three centuries ago, the recognized leader of the community of the city of Safed, Its'chak Luria, was walking with his disciples to the synagogue at the beginning of Shabbat, the day of rest and prayer. On the way, he suggested to them that

---

* The Wisdom of the Zohar - I. Tishbi, Vol. II

they spend Saturday in Jerusalem. The city of Jerusalem lay three days' journey from Safed; soon he was asked, "But what are you talking about? How can we spend Saturday in Jerusalem, three days journey away from here? We'll never arrive in time!" Luria replied, "If you had not doubted, we would be walking in the streets of Jerusalem right now!"

What was Luria talking about? What access did he have to this other place, so far away? Was he talking about vehicles such as those we have today, which conquer time with speed, cutting the trip to 15 minutes? Or was this an allusion to imagination, which can take us wherever we want? According to Jewish mystical tradition, neither of these interpretations is correct. Luria knew *K'fitsat ha-derech*, the shortcut that turns any and every place, into any other and every other place.

The concept defined in Jacob's experience, which is also present in the idea of jumping the path, is that portals-- *shaarim*-- exist in places. But before we speak of these portals, embodied today in the Internet model, we will first try to understand the concept of windows --or Windows, as Microsoft has it. Like portals, windows set up contact with other spaces. But windows are instruments or applications for perceiving what lies beyond, while portals allow us to go beyond. To understand how to go beyond, we must first think about what that beyond is. Windows help in this sense.

WINDOWS 2030

Quite soon after I received an invitation to the launch of Microsoft Corp.'s Windows Millennium software, a great cybernetic event of the times, a very dear master, Reb Zalman Schachter, came to Rio for a visit. The invitation had been on my desk for a few days when, on the eve of the master's arrival, I had a dream. It was one of those sweet dreams that provide a sense of absolute peace and euphoria, even after the sleeper awakens.

I dreamt I was standing in a place when an old man came up to me. I looked at him closely, curious, and saw that I knew him. "Aren't you the Baal Shem Tov?" I asked, incredulous. The Baal Shem Tov is the most important Jewish spiritual leader of the late 18th century, maybe even of the entire modern era. He answered with a simple unaffected, "Yes."

I still remember the great joy and excitement I felt. "I have something for you..." -- he went on -- "something that no other human being possesses." I felt deeply blessed, or maybe to be more honest to the feeling, I felt like a child ready to receive a long-awaited gift that no other child in the neighborhood has. I thought, "What could it be that no human being has?" As if he had read my thoughts, the Baal Shem Tov answered immediately,. "I am going to give you Windows' 2030."

I awoke feeling a mixture of well-being and humor. Wasn't this incredibly wise, on the part of my unconscious? Give me something no one else has... how would I get out of this one? My unconscious came up with quite a creative response. Windows, in the form of the invitation still hovering around my desk, was

11

the answer. But not just any Windows, not even the Millennium version; this any mortal could obtain. This was the Windows that did not exist yet, but would one day come to exist.

The Baal Shem Tov offered me something that could not be obtained, except with the passing of the time that separates what will one day be available to us all, from what is today a mere speculation of the mind. This is what I thought at first. But then I paid attention to the metaphor of Windows itself and began to realize that my unconscious had played quite a sophisticated trick on me.

The Baal Shem Tov brought my attention to the fact that Windows '2030 is not reached only with the passage of time, but that it would be enough to open windows, even through Windows' Millenium. Thus access becomes available to what would otherwise remain out of reach. Windows, unlike doors, do not take us to another place, but allow us to see another place.

The Microsoft software is nothing more than a means which allow us to integrate our work, by way of the medium of windows that open and overlay. By superimposing several windows from different workplaces onto a single one, we gain levels of efficiency that were previously unattainable.

When I told my dream to the master the following day, he surprised me by recommending a teaching of the Baal Shem Tov which I had never read. They were the words of the Baal Shem Tov, from two centuries ago, on the medium of windows.

WINDOWS 1751

Ein chadash tachat ha-shamesh... There is nothing extraordinarily new under the sun, says the book of Ecclesiastics, He-who-knows. What is always new are the applications, the way knowledge can be put to use for humans and humanity. From this perspective, patents and copyrights make sense only for applications. Otherwise, Microsoft would have to find the descendants of the Baal Shem Tov and recognize his precedence, in the creation of the windows medium, at least 200 years before.

In the teaching my master suggested, there was an amazing connection with my dream. The theme of the Baal Shem Tov's teaching was about the role of prayer and liturgy, as a medium. Wondering how a sacred text should be treated, he cited a verse from the Bible in Genesis (5:16). The context of this verse is the story of Noah. G-d recommends the building of an ark, --*tevah*-- so Noah could survive the flood together with the animals he was to collect. Among these recommendations, we find: *tsoar ta'asseh la-tevah*-- thou shall build a window/opening for thy ark. The Baal Shem Tov then makes an incredible connection. The word *tevah* in Hebrew, used in the sense of ark, also means vocable, or word. Thus what is a word is also an ark, a vessel containing a sign or meaning preserved inside it. A word is a ship.

But this was not the great insight of the Baal Shem Tov. He then returns to the verse of Genesis for a new reading, with the meaning of *tevah* as vocable. The verse is read as follows: "Make

13

a window for your word." The Baal Shem Tov then explained that words and their literal meanings are merely "arks/ships" for which we must know how to open windows. These windows reveal what is behind words. We thus discover that words are media and that, far beyond their concrete meanings, they allow us to open a series of new dimensions sparked by them, so as to widen our comprehension and horizons.

The windows we use visually today, in the form of screens superimposed on each other, the grand graphic idea of the Windows program, were imagined 200 years ago by the Baal Shem Tov. He certainly understood that each word can be a site, a point on a web spreading out to other points, turning a liturgical text or the Bible itself into a point of departure to all corners of the universe -- a talk with the Creator.

Even though he did not have the medium (hardware) to contemplate his idea visually, the Baal Shem Tov conceived a kind of relationship one should have with a prayer text that is very similar to the basic concept of the well-known computer program, Windows.

How much did people know in the past about that which our technological tools of today are allowing us to experience? The search for that answer can bring us to fascinating discoveries.

THE FIRST INTERACTIVE PAGE

Jewish tradition has always distinguished itself by giving great value to media, the means used to transmit culture and heritage. The Torah was transmitted by way of the most sophisticated medium of the time, writing. The Scriptures used letters printed in stone and on papyrus. Hardware, no matter how rudimentary, was exploited to its fullest, through the concept of a text that says what it says and also says what it does not say. This was the beginning of not only text, but commentary.

Yet it was almost a millennium later, with the compilation of the Talmud, that a fantastic innovation was added to the medium for passing on tradition. The Talmud is a monumental work, both in size and in audacity, where the rabbis registered the oral tradition that was not part of the Biblical Scriptures. Still using hardware similar to that of the Torah, the Talmud was conceived as the first interactive page in human history. On one *daf* (hypertext page), there are windows for commentators from different generations and centuries (see illustration), relating to a fixed, main text. These are dialogues among individuals who lived in different eras, who never met in the physical world, but did meet in the virtual world set up by the Talmud. And the footnotes and margins (tools) of each page offer cross-references, permitting the reader to link up one issue dealt with in the Talmud, with other textual sources, or with the Bible.

The Talmud is an extremely advanced piece of graphic design, providing the simultaneous opening of several "screens" (windows) that can be overlaid. The medium here gives us not

15

only the commentary, but commentary on the commentary. Thus it is possible to keep pace with the mental process itself, the decoding and commenting.

A person who connects with the Talmud gets as enthusiastic as today's interactive pages user, accessing countless windows. Without leaving his page, he can access minds of the past, from different eras. One mind can lead to another, one question to another. The fantastic web that is woven arises not only from the content of the text, but from the novel formatting which gave a new dimension to the text itself.

The medium is fundamental to understanding not just the content of a text or piece of information, but also the context in which these are expressed.

Sample of Talmud page

PART II

PORTALS

THE TECHNOLOGY OF BEING, WITHOUT BEING IN A PLACE

At the start of the Common Era, the people of Israel underwent a catastrophic experience. For more than a century and a half, the Roman invasion threatened to wipe out not only the Hebrews' sovereignty, but their very culture and civilization. The eschatologies preaching the world's end by way of various phenomena truly reflected a real sense of imminent catastrophe, and this ultimately took place in the year 135 A.D. Israel suffered a defeat resulting from its last attempt to throw off the Roman yoke, 65 years after losing the Temple, the greatest symbol of its tradition. Thus began the longest exile of a people in the entire history of East and West, an exile of more than 1,800 years.

For those who experienced this period, there was no doubt; it was long enough to be lived as if the world were ending. What is particularly interesting here is the fact that this group tried to stay together, without a national homeland. In a world yet to develop the concepts of nation and state, when most modern states were no more than feudal groupings, a cohesive nation was losing its place despite great cultural vitality. Losing the land, with its fruits and landscape, its climate, language and culture, was like a soul losing a body; and this produced a feeling of imminent finality.

Nevertheless, in this century and a half of Roman domination, the sages of Israel sought ways to save this nation. One image that helps to bring back the feelings of this time is the famous comic strip hero, Superman. This hero, created by a Jew between

21

the two world wars, featured the life of a survivor of a dying world (Europe). The start of the Superman series shows the sages of his home planet preparing for the end. A scientist couple sends their son, their seed, to another world (America) in a ship, to flee his own disintegrating world.

Their attempt to rescue a sole specimen was no doubt easier than it must have been for the rabbis to save a culture that is beyond the individual level and the fruit of collective interactions. How was it possible to put a culture and its civilization into a ship, a lifeboat?

Unlike the planet Krypton or even the sinking Atlantis, the issue here was not just the physical survival of a people without a place, but collective virtual survival. Because cohesion could no longer come from meeting in one place, the challenge was to find a way to be together without being in one place.

Over and over again, this experience has marked the sons of Israel. They became a people without a place, a nation of virtual existence.

A Jewish joke shows how this relation with non-place lasted up until only a few decades ago. The story is that in Nazi Germany, when Jewish emigration was almost totally shut down, a Jew went to a travel agency to buy a ticket in a ship, so he could flee. At the agency, they asked where he wanted to go. He said he had no preference, any place was fine. The agent insisted that he decide, otherwise how could he sell the ticket? The Jew then asked for a globe sitting on the counter, and began to point to different places in the hope of finding a safe port. But for every country he pointed to, he heard the same sort of explanation. "Here, they don't take any more Jewish immigrants... in this one the immigration quota has been reached....," After a while, the man pathetically asked, "Don't you have another globe?"

Transcending the dimension of place came to be a survival task for the Jews. And doing this collectively is an unusual mission. How is it possible to be networked if not by way of spatial connections?

A PLACE MADE OF TEXT

Every crisis demands some form of detachment from the past, and simultaneously, a synthesis of the past. The intellectual elite of the rabbis perceived this. Just as today's corporate executives creatively react to the market's dynamics with brainstorming sessions, the rabbis projected possible scenarios for their people's future.

The first step in terms of detachment from the past took place in a episode with Rabbi Yochanan ben Zakkai. During the 70 A.D. Roman siege leading to the partial destruction of Jerusalem and the total destruction of the Second Temple, Ben Zakkai came (through a series of events which need not be related here) before the general in charge. Able to foresee that this man would become emperor, he charmed him into allowing a favor. Amazingly, in the middle of a siege on the physical heart of his people's culture, Ben Zakkai does not ask to spare Jerusalem. His request, to History's indignation, is for a small place called Yavne. Ben Zakkai wants a permission to create a rabbinical academy there.

Ben Zakkai was exchanging a place beyond comparison for a symbolic location. In Yavne, this locale of temporary importance, Ben Zakkai made possible the establishment of a think-tank --the creative center-- of a virtual nation. Here was the founding of a place unrelated to space. But what place was this?

In Yavne, a government with a term of more than 1,800 years was set up. It had executive, legislative and judicial branches, with the legitimacy of their authority ruling not over a national territory, but over a national text. The synthesis of the past would happen in Yavne with the compilation of a pocket territory: the Mishnah, which together with the Gemara, would come to be the Talmud.

In the words of the poet-philosopher Derrida, "The house of the Jew and of the poet is text... the 'motherland of the Jews' is a sacred text surrounded by commentary". Like the poet who opens windows and allows portals, a nation transported its territory to the pocket medium of the times, the book.

Actually, the sages who composed the Talmud used millenary experience with Biblical text, that gave them the insight and confidence in the idea that a text could delimit a territory and contain a nation. A text could have the efficiency of an executive who implements laws, could legislate like a national assembly, and could arbitrate like a national tribunal. To live within the frontiers of text, organized and managed by it, was to live in a place that could be any place. Being able to access the text meant keeping a whole nation together, no matter how far it spread to the four corners of the globe. And if you want to be part of the people of Israel, all you have to do is grab your medium --the Talmud-- and connect yourself with your text provider in a place that is not the same as where you are.

Limited only by the pace at which information could be exchanged, the rabbis of subsequent generations updated the Talmud with new commentary, new sites and home-pages. They reached the server, the editors of the Talmud pages, by letter or manuscripts showing the results of the thinking done by communities in France, North Africa, or Italy. Without going to Italy or France, a member of the Hebrew nation had access to a meeting place that was not a physical place, but the inside of a text. A place made of text came into being.

Ben Zakkai was the first to work with the idea of the word contained in the Biblical canon as a virtual dimension. A word is a window, and incredibly, it can also be a portal. The Bible carried in itself the seed that G-d is not in any place. He is not in a pagan statue, nor in a place in the Temple. His house is in a place here and every place, but is neither this place here nor every place as we perceive it.

Almost two thousand years ago, Ben Zakkai traded place -- Jerusalem-- for a non-place, Yavne. The place, Jerusalem, went two thousand years as a non-place, abandoned and desolate. The paradigm of place remained however, and Jerusalem emerges today as the symbol of place, the place. Perhaps the great transcendence of this paradigm of place as physical place to a paradigm of a place that allows windows and can serve as a portal, is the symbolic role that this place Jerusalem will have in the future of Western history.

Of course, the dream of these near two millennia has been a return to Jerusalem. The draw of the earth, of merely physical space, will one day be remembered as a behavior of the masses, similar to the fall of the Hebrews leaving Egypt, when they worshipped the golden calf. Notably, anguish and doubt have marked the return to the physical Jerusalem. More than a few have spoken out, saying that the sought-after Jerusalem is no longer the earthly Jerusalem, but the heavenly one. This virtual Jerusalem could no longer be confused with the place where G-d is. Heavenly Jerusalem would be the place that is not a place, which is a portal, like the ancient view of Jerusalem as the navel of the world, the connection between earth and the heavens. We recall the catharsis of Jacob -- this place is but a door to the heavens, the heavens that are the physical place where the ancients projected their understanding of the metaphysical.

Ultimately, the survival of the Jews for this long period came in large part from the transformation of place into poem, from setting up a link that, in daily life, did not happen in the place where they where. It happened, above all, in the texts.

A PLACE MADE OF TIME

In making a synthesis of the past, the sages of Yavne were seeking directions on how to proceed toward the future while anticipating the very changes it would bring. Since text was an element so much a part of this culture that it could become "place", substituting a physical place, the sages asked themselves if there might be another element as intrinsic to this tradition, that could also function as a place, to substitute a particular place?

In turning to their own culture, the sages found one more possibility: time. Their culture based on cyclical time revolved around a chronology going from the first day to the seventh, and starting over at the first. There was no eighth day. After Saturday, the seventh day, comes a return to Sunday, the first day. Saturday-- the Sabbath-- is the day G-d rests in Israel's theology and mythology. Where does He rest? What place is this that G-d rests? He rests in time.

The sages thus began to invest even more in this notion. After all, the people of Israel would have no longer a Jerusalem to meet in, nor a Temple in which to congregate. They would thus come to congregate in time. In this way, the Sabbath was turned into a meeting place. In this corner of the earth, or some other, whoever was experiencing *shabbat* would be in Jewish territory. This is the concept that led the contemporary philosopher Abraham Heschel to call the Sabbath a cathedral in time.

For the Jews of the Diaspora, a cathedral in time is more of a place for prayer and study, than it ever was in ancient times. In Biblical Israel, the Sabbath appears more as a social and ethical idea. Allowing a rest means respecting the world's biorhythm, the right thing to do both in terms of human solidarity and a harmonious relationship with the environment. For the rabbis after Yavne, the Sabbath became more than this. The Sabbath is a day of being on-line. It is a tool of virtual congregation.

The Sabbath represented the ancient discovery that the heart of existence is time, and that human beings use this time to conquer space. Place is perceived by human beings as the most concrete representation of concrete possession and conquest and it can only be achieved by consuming time. The Biblical notion of rest revealed the cost we know today so well by way of ecological imbalances, caused by our unceasing activity towards the conquest of place. The Yavne rabbis added to this notion the idea that taking refuge in the Sabbath, turning it into a virtual place, would be therapeutic in the discovery of another kind of space conquest.

Human relations with territory have always been an animal source of dispute and aggressiveness. To take refuge in time allows for the experience of time as a territory and thus provides us a much more real sense of its finiteness. An individual's limits of time are much more easily perceived than his limits of space. Limits on space, on territory, only came to be known some 500 years ago, with the discovery of the true dimensions of this planet, and more recently, with pollution and ecology as measures of space saturation. Limits on time, in the other hand, are as old as human consciousness of life span.

The rabbis knew that time could be a virtual place and the verb "to be" would come to define some sort of co-existence, of togetherness. Anyone in time, no matter how far away, is accessible. To create a cathedral in time meant opening a roof, a connection over all others, regardless of location, an inter-linked network, which provided a chance to be without necessarily being in the same place.

THE FIRST NET

The notion that a great network awaits our accessing it might be even more ancient than we may suppose. The concept of prayer to the Creator, for exempla, comes from a primitive understanding that some portal, that some server, represented by a religious tradition, could connect us directly with this network. Once in contact with it, we could navigate it individually.

This concept derives solely from the idea that everything is inter-linked. The idea of monotheism was a major step in expressing of that concept. The oneness of G-d does not allow for the understanding of something as "external"; on the contrary, everything is seen as part of an integrated reality. In the Ethic of the Ancestors* (3:20) we encounter the word "net" mentioned as to convey this very idea:

"Rabi Akiva used to say, 'All is offered to us, but not unconditionally. And the net is open over all that lives. The store is open, the shopkeeper offers everything on credit, the account book is open, and his hand makes notes in it, and anyone who wants to make use of this may come and do it; and the collectors make their shifts continually, and receive their payments, volunteered or not, as they have promissory notes. And the balance is an absolute balance and all this makes the banquet possible.'"*

Every place is a site, a point that exists in a connection, a network. In this great supermarket of the universe, where we exchange the possibility of our own existence, the banquet is

---

* Book that is part of the Mishnah, section II

only possible by way of this absolute interaction of everything with everything. Our discoveries in the field of ecology are very interesting in this sense. When did the West discover the existence of a balance on which we depend on? It was only possible when we were able set up connections between places. Before, we thought that trash thrown in a certain place, or smoke produced in a certain place, were not a question of concern if we lived somewhere else. An extinct forest here, or a species that disappears here, did not seem to have the slightest effect there. This is a great mistake!

Everything is a site on this great network. A dwindling panda population affects the whole chain of life on the Earth. The pandas are not relevant solely to their habitat, because pandas are a connection, a portal with here. We may take a long time to realize this, but it is real. It is so real that the extinction of apparently unimportant species have begun to influence our lives exponentially. This discovery of the ecosystem was only possible because we were able to measure the interconnection of one place with other places by their being on-line.

And what do we know of what lies beyond the maps of our planet? There are places in profusion in this universe and not only outside ourselves. Here within us there are places, microscopic ones, but places. The day we discover all the dimensions of a place, we will discover that what we seek today by way of ecology and the "cure" of our planet, the network we perceive as sustaining us, greatly transcends the responsibility of this tiny piece of the net.

This was what the prophets meant with their warnings, which translated to us in the sphere of ethics: "You are unbalancing networks!" This is also what is meant by the primeval warning described in the Ethic of the Ancestors (2:1): "Know what is beyond! An Eye that sees; an Ear that hears; and all is registered." Our religious traditions say this many times in forms that have become banal, but the origin of this perception, renewed in each generation that experiences existence, is that there is a "beyond" here. This place here has an Eye and an Ear; it is a portal to the Net. This is the Eye/Ear that makes Jacob say, "Surely the Lord is in the place and I knew it not."

God that is here but not here is the essence of the Net.

For Jewish tradition, access to G-d, the Absolute Net, can come in three ways: insight, prayer, and just (attuned) attitude. Jacob's insight, for exempla, allowed him to discover layers of places in one given place, or as we would say a site of a net. Just (attuned) attitudes -- translated as *tsedakah* -- represent the possibility of function within the net's parameters, in an intuitive fashion. To know how to be just, understanding dimensions not only of human laws and duties, but also of the Eye/Ear of the Net, is to function within it. But as for prayer we might need some more explanation.

Earlier, in the section on Windows 1751, we saw that the Baal Shem Tov perceived that words, especially those of a prayer, could be windows. G-d tells Noah to build windows for his words. But do these windows provide contact with the world they reveal? Can something be passed or sent through a window?

The Biblical text can takes even further in its metaphor when it states: "(by the window) he sent a dove." Noah sends a dove to see if there is a place to make port in this great no-place-flood. The fact that the dove is able to arrive in a place makes into a portal what was at a given moment a mere window. The rabbis say symbolically, "Prayers, they themselves do not have wings. They must be carried to the heavens (no-place). And how do they fly thus? They fly on the wings of a dove, as it is written, 'and by the window he sent a dove.' Every generation needs its own dove to carry its prayers to the angel Sandalfon, the angel who weaves (in the net) these prayers and lace and plaits that the Eternal, Blessed be He, uses on His Throne." These words made in windows, in the windows of the experience of prayer, are put on the wings of doves that are meant to take to the Great

31

Provider, to the Universal Wide Web (UWW), where the net is knitted and put onto a universal link.

Obviously, this is a figurative reading, with the use of the language of our times. But might this reading be a figment of our imagination? Perhaps we are dealing with something that is real? What did the ancients mean anyway, with all these metaphors and symbols, coded in language?

To answer these questions, we should perhaps delve even more into the metaphors. It might be of interest to better understand the "dove" as a tool. How was this "dove" experienced in ancient practice?

According to Jewish tradition, there is a specific way to send prayers made by each individual, in his or her Windows, in the windows open to liturgy. What way is this? The *mynian*, the minimum required quorum for community prayer. For Jews, a prayer is only strong enough to get to the throne if there is a quorum of ten. With fewer than ten people, prayer is possible, but this kind of prayer is an opening of windows, not a portal. This is why we often see people outside a synagogue trying to find enough participants to send a "new message" through a portal to heaven. Ten people allow access to a non-place on a collective level, not just individually.

We comprehend something important here: our minds and imaginations are not portals, but windows. We can be anywhere, or jump the path, in our imaginations. But the fact that this is non-interactive with other places or with the "other", makes it a window-tool. Individual prayer is a window, and can be of great value in harmonizing thought, feeling and action in the world, with what one sees through the window. But the individual is not there. Prayers do not have wings. To be there, to be transported, prayer needs a dove, a portal where collective "being" is in a non-place. This is very complex. The net is not a net until it is used collectively. The Internet itself is a non-place only when many people are interacting there. Without interaction, it is a non-place, but no one can be in it.

Being in a non-place is only possible with a lot of other people. Collective experience configures nets and once this happens many incredible things can take place.

The *mynian* is thus a net port, as conceived in primitive times. As part of one, an individual can have his prayers raised to heaven, to a non-place, transported on wings. The *mynian* is a server, where everyone who gets on line can send and receive mail.

I reiterate here that the use of this language is not meant to claim that Judaism or religious tradition foresaw what the present and the future are now revealing to us, by way of its applications. What I deeply believe is that intuitively and existentially, relating to a place as the place or a non-place, is very ancient, as ancient as human consciousness. What was a gas lamp? It was a light bulb. Of course people in the era of gaslight did not experience electricity, but their firelight is similar to the friction of electrons in the wiring of a light bulb. They did not know electricity, but they wanted to conquer the dark with light, and knowledge of this was as primeval as consciousness of the sun.

A *mynian* is a net. This is not because people who have experienced prayer both with and without a quorum note a difference, but because the *mynian* was intuitively conceived as a net. The *mynian* was also an invention of rabbis who sought virtual Judaism. In the absence of a Temple with its complex ritual meant to primitively ascend to the dimension of G-d, a port for words was set up, a place of departures and arrivals that was not a physical place. What came to represent the Temple was in no way the synagogue, but the *mynian*. In any place where ten or more people position themselves to access the net, a connection is possible. Those who do not perceive this possibility may think that this whole process of prayer is a waste of time and a serious manifestation of poor taste. They are wrong, of course.

After all, a mother may shout to her son on the Internet, "Come out of there, you've been in that room all day!" Leaving aside the pros and cons of anti-social behavior, this young man was not just in his room. He went far. He traveled to places his mother will probably never see, or that he himself may never come to physically experience. This will certainly be one of the most difficult things for human beings to get used to-- not having to actually be in a place.

The actual not being in a place is usually experienced as detached from reality. We have come to view this as the world of imagination, of non-interaction. We are, however, dealing here with a different level of not being in a specific place. It has to do with not being there but at the same time interacting with everything that seems there and much more. One of the characteristics of illusion is the fact that it is a partial, an individual, presentation of reality. There is no interaction in illusion. We may even say that there is sharing in illusion but there is no open communication between illusion and reality. Virtuality, on the other hand, cannot exist if not in the realm of interaction. This is what makes it so incredible as a concept. We know for fact that reality is no other than the quintessential shared experience. Its essence though is of virtuality. It is a virtuality that your car, your table and your fellow humans can share with you, but if taken in absolute terms is of virtual nature. The wheel of your car thinks that the ground is hard and may react physically experiencing let say the inertia. But the ground is not necessarily hard in absolute terms. What it is I don't know, all I can attest is that shared experience of virtuality had made it real as being hard.

What makes a portal is the capability that people have for sharing the views that their windows can provide them. The more the views are shared, the more these windows are common to all, the easier it is to open a door and step outside into a new landscape. That which was once empty and perceived as void, it is now made firm and allows for steps where no human has ever been before.

KABBALAH AND PORTALS

That which we are describing, the turning of walls into windows and windows into doors, is the very task of the Kabbalist. Long ago the Kabbalists realized that they could depart from the text (they used the sacred biblical text for that purpose) and recreate a new reality. They could do this as long they were able to share there perceptions, as long as they could communicate with other human beings and have them partake of these perceptions.

In psychology, associations are used as a way of revealing concealed symbols of our unconsciousness. Once they are revealed they can account for a broader understanding of our lives. When however more than one individual can make the same associations that gets upgraded to the level of revealing concealed data about humankind's nature. Imagine now that we can create a "therapy" session where everything could make associations between things that would seem otherwise with no connection. This would reveal concealed data and possibilities of the order of reality itself. We don't usually believe that because we are constantly seduced by the status quo of our perceptions. It happens in the social arena, for exempla, where a specific mentality might need decades to sink into a culture. But once it does, once a critic mass of individuals perceive something in a specific way, it becomes part of reality and interacts with it as being "real".

To our absolute perplexity that also happens in the physical world. That which is heavier than the air falls, however, the airplane is heavier than the air and it flies. It is true that it never changed the reality of gravity, to the opposite, it merely attests to that reality. When applying speed and aerodynamics forms the push upwards might be bigger then the force of gravity and something heavier than the air can be lifted. Speed and aerodynamics are accesses to that which cannot be experienced in exposure to the law of gravity alone. "Heavier than the air falls" is the here, "airplanes, which are heavier than the air can fly", is the there. The interconnectedness of the here and there is made by the doors that allowed human beings to master the possibility of flying. To sum it up, "heavier than air cannot fly" is a wall, laws of physics that envision flying are windows and the actual being at 33.000 feet above the ocean in a 767 is undoubtedly having crossed a door.

Kabbalist would meet at night to talk about their discoveries. Daylight could not contain their dream like discoveries. All night long they would make connections and interpretations creating links between that which would seem at first sight disconnected. The more radical the disconnections that were linked and the more they could be shared with others the more magical their achievements were. They were carpenters of a different dimension. They provided windows to worlds that were until then unseen. The wider the windows the more daring they were in creating doors.

The alchemists were merely an extreme expression of that belief. You can certainly attract people's attention when it comes to state that there is a door from stone to gold. Talking of practical application for theories certainly stroke as a most justifiable pursue. But it comes only to serve as an example of the incredible world that allows us to go from here to there. All you need is an interactive access, a *minyan*, a collective window.

PRIMITIVE KIT FOR SERVER LINKUP

Yet another metaphor remains to be discussed if we are to understand the work of the rabbis in the area of virtuality. It has to do with an important yet strange ritual object that we find in Jewish tradition. Many religions have objects to aid concentration in prayer. There are vestments and shawls, or objects made of natural materials, such as animal horn, whistles carved from bird bones, and many more. The objects to which I refer in Jewish tradition are the *tefilin*, or phylacteries. Their name defines them well, coming from the same root as the verb "to pray". Perhaps we can translate them as "prayor", a praying kit.

What is most strange about the *tefilin* is that they are not objects from nature, or a sort of vestment to distinguish kings, priests or sages. The *tefilin* are gadgets. In a rather sophisticated manner, they are made of wooden leather boxes tied to leather strips (see figure). One box is tied to the left arm near the heart, and the other to the head, so the box sits on the forehead right between the eyes.

The phylactery placed on the arm is rolled seven times around the forearm, and also around the fingers, so as to spell the Hebrew letters *shin*, *dalet* and *yud*. These letters are the initials of the phrase "Guardian of the Gates of Israel" (*shomer d'latot israel*). This could be no other way; G-d is the password, the Guardian, to access at all portals.

Inside these boxes is the most amazing aspect of the *tefilin*: text. Like *pen drives* or *flash drives* crafted in the Stone Age (not disks, but cubes, actually), the *tefilin* boxes carry a small software program to be loaded every morning in the life of a Jew. Again, this would be no more than a caricature interpretation, if not for the contents of the "software".

Jews are to wear the *tefilin* as a sign, a way to recall their life commitments. As you start your day, you must remember who you are and what you believe. Every day, all of us act on impulse or without thinking, out of tune with our own interests and wishes. The *tefilin* are a way to harmonize both feelings (the box close to the heart) and thoughts (box close to the brain), providing a sense of direction and balance.

But what is the content of this software, of the texts inserted in the *pen drives*? We find in them the fundamental assertion of Jewish liturgy (Deut. 6:4): Hear(Connect yourself) O Israel, the Lord is God, the Lord is One", and other Biblical passages, where the use of the *tefilin* is mentioned. One of these passages, perhaps the most important, also comes from Deuteronomy (11:13-21). It begins with the same verb "hear/connect oneself", and carries a tone of warning.

"If ye shall hearken diligently unto my commandments which I command you this day, to love the Lord your God, and to serve him with all your heart and with your soul, that I will give you the rain of your land in his due season, the first rain and the latter rain, that thou mayest gather in thy corn, and thy wine, and thy oil. And I will send grass in the thy fields for thy cattle, that thou mayest eat and be full. Take heed to yourselves, that your heart not be deceived, and ye turn aside, and serve other gods, and worship them; and then the Lord's wrath be kindled against you, and he shut up the heaven, that there be no rain, and that the land yield not her fruit; and lest ye perish quickly from off the good land which the Lord giveth you."

This text is not a divine threat. It does not warn of a punishment, but of the consequences of a particular behavior. Before ecological consciousness, few people understood that a corruption here or an act of disrespect there could cause rain to fall at the wrong time, and keep the fields from producing at the right time. Of course, a pragmatic person thinks there is no relationship between rain and our acts. But the truth is that all of our problems with pollution and environmental destruction come from petty diversions, the thefts, evils and greed of our history. And what the ancients could not possibly know as proven fact is written in Deuteronomy. How could they know of this?

They knew because they understood the principle of a place that is a non-place. They did not even know the earth is round or finite, but they knew that there are connections among all things and that the nets, though not visible or perceptible, are out there happening in different dimensions.

The *tefilin* are impressive objects because they are similar in format to diskettes of old or *pen drives* and they work as if their users "loaded" the program, the "software" installed inside them. And a person who uses *tefilin* can attest that their use is exactly this, as if he were putting this text into his unconscious every morning, as the first act of the day. His aim is to make a connection with the net that can last all day in his interactions with the world.

Leather, rolled up like in a bobbin, does not "conduct" energy, the way electricity travels. Perhaps we can say figuratively that the idea of these gadgets is not to "conduct" or lead to any place in particular. It is that place, the place where one is, that must be activated in all its portals.

The *tefilin* and the *mynian* are resources of a liturgical tradition that views the act of prayer as a search for a portal, an access to a larger net stretching far beyond our ability to perceive a given place. They function, respectively, as a program and connection "kit", and a server for getting on line.

Nilton Bonder

According to the Tractate of *Berachot* on the Talmud, G-d himself puts on *tefilin* very day. In a way it alludes to the possibility of universal access -- of everything with everything. And that is what the idea of a net is all about.

PART III

THE NEW PARADIGM OF PLACE
A SITE

HEAVENLY JERUSALEM

Jerusalem is the heart of the paradigm of place. No other place in the West has lasted so long as a symbol of power through place. This has nothing to do with being a place coveted for its treasures, since no one ever conquered it for this reason, nor is the city a place that represented political power such as Rome or Alexandria were. Jerusalem was the place where the founding events of the major Western religions occurred. These three religions-- Judaism, Christianity, and Islam -- grew out of the culture of the people of Israel, who had chosen Jerusalem as a place above all others. Although Rome became the center of Christianity, and Mecca, the center of Islam, these two places symbolically reproduce the meaning of Jerusalem as The Place. This city was chosen not merely because it was an economic, political and spiritual center, but because its own mythology put it at the center of the earth. Ancient maps were made to show the earth converging at this spot. The Hebrews started the custom of turning their prayers to this location, making it into a cosmic focal point. The Moslem world also came to do this with Mecca, but the original meaning comes from the concept of Jerusalem.

Even the dispute which has characterized the city's history, the violence of which lives on into our days, illustrates the role it plays. There is a place, the place, and whoever possesses it is in the place.

On my most recent visit to the place, Jerusalem, I came upon a striking scene. It was a Moslem holy day and the mosque area, an ancient place where the Temples of Jerusalem were erected, was crowded with a quarter of a million Muslims. At a certain moment, from the Jewish quarter of the old city, here is what I saw: Jews on the outside, praying to the Wailing Wall, Muslims at prayer on top of the hill, and in the distance, churches with their towers and the sound of bells.

A strange insight came to me. Looking from above, from the perspective of the G-d to whom these people pray, there is no difference between the Messianic times of absolute harmony and the times we live in, of confrontation and conflict among these religious traditions. The dream, the utopia that permeates these three civilizations is not only to be found in the future, but right here, in this place, in another place. I stood before what the prophets said: here is another way of seeing reality. There is a utopia just as virtual as that which we so commonly raise to the level of reality. This way of seeing is the total distance that exists between what is possible and impossible in this place. The doors exist, and if they open for several individuals, these people will start to be in another place, which is the non-place of this place. This possibility is still incomprehensible to most of us.

Still, the seed of understanding about this non-place has existed since ancient times. In Jewish tradition, there were two different Jerusalems. One was the *shel-mata*, lower Jerusalem, and the other was the *shel-mala*, upper Jerusalem. The heavenly city was the inverse image of the terrestrial city. The absolute and definite construction of this city would take place when the terrestrial Jerusalem merged with the celestial Jerusalem. The fusion of this place with the non-place would produce the effect described by the prophet Isaiah (2:3): "...out of Zion shall go forth the Torah, and the word of G-d from Jerusalem."

The notion of mobility, the words "shall go forth", are striking for a paradigm of place. Why not say that the Torah and the word will be in Jerusalem? Because in its least superficial conception, the place Jerusalem is a door through which this

Torah and this word will be heard and perceived. This is no longer a Jerusalem to which one goes, but a Jerusalem that comes to us -- a Jerusalem that is not there, but here, "any here".

An item of great importance in this Jerusalem-place was doubtless the Temple, the center of the center. Actually, the most important place of all was the center of the center... of the center. Jerusalem had its center in the Temple, and the Temple's center was the *kodesh-ha-kodashim*, the Sanctum Sanctorum. This absolute place was a room where the Tablets of the Law, the original Torah, were kept. The Great Temple had in its center a box similar to the *tefilin* boxes, the greatest monument of access to the Great Net. The Temple was the symbolic center of connection between this world below, with the absolute universe. And of course, the Hebrews bowed only before this symbol, a cube containing human beings' most important software. This software, this access program, was the Torah. In other words, the main architectural symbol of this cosmic Temple was the "disk", the collective *tefilin* for access to the absolute non-place where G-d lives -- where He is, was and will be.

In the Hebrews' center of the world, there was an umbilical cord, a portal between terrestrial Jerusalem and celestial Jerusalem (between Jerusalem-place and Jerusalem any-place). And that non-place known as the Holy of Holies was visited once a year on the day of Yom Kippur by the High Priest. This was the most important symbolic moment stemming from the archaic idea that this universe is a net connected not by space nor by time, but by portals of access. Yom Kippur has more to teach us about portals.

THE CULT OF PORTALS
AND THE MASTER PASSWORD

What is Yom Kippur? It is a different day from other holidays. While all other festivals are either linked to the agricultural calendar, or to historic events, Yom Kippur is a day of the individual. Its structure centers on the cult of the portal. The day's entire symbolism is marked by the idea that a "portal" will open for a brief interval and that we must be able to connect in this time. Its entire liturgy is devoted to the idea of linking oneself and reaching a connection status with the Creator. The end of Yom Kippur, the most fervent religious service of the Jewish liturgical calendar, is no other then the *Neilah*, the "Closing of the Portals". The main idea is, therefore, that you may not let those portals to close, without having achieved access through them.

The portals of justice, health, sustenance, compassion, wisdom and peace are just a few of those that can be accessed via the Yom Kippur connection. Anything that is disconnected from this moment and this place -- health that cannot be regained, for example, or wisdom that is too distant -- all this is accessible by jumping the path, when these portals are open. I will not delve into theology to explain how it is possible to jump over something, when this is apparently impossible, even from our most sophisticated perception of reality. In the sermons of my rabbinical practice, I always point out that there are no shortcuts in the process of personal growth. We must walk the entire path, because *"caminante... el camino se hace al andar"*, as a Spanish saying tells us; in walking we make the path.

How then, is it possible to jump the path, without evoking here the darkness of ignorance or an alienating ingenuousness? The difference is that here, we are talking not about shortcuts, but about being here, being there. Later, we will spend some time with the question of discontinuities. What is important at this stage is that sharpened sensibility ought not to be confused with ego and manipulations of will. The portals are not shortcuts, they are exactly what they are; passing through them, here becomes there.

In ancient times, this day of Kippur was preceded by a complex process of purification for the High Priest (today experienced as ten days of concentration). This process of baths and meditations, of instructions from other sages, was undertaken to allow the High Priest to face the culminating moment of Yom Kippur, his entrance to the Sanctum Sanctorum. Tied by a rope so he could be pulled back in case of an accident or another kind of problem, the High Priest was the only person who could enter this place, and then only once a year. He was entering a place-non-place and that was why he had to be tied, since what was here could end there and no one from here could go there to get what comes from here.

But what was the priest doing in the here that is there? The idea was that he would bring back with him the knowledge of the password of master access to the Absolute Net. He would come out with the "explicit" Name of G-d, the password of the Tetragrammaton, **** (YHWH), which was made revealed to the High Priest and no other on that day, in that very place-non-place. According to the tradition of the Hebrews, the High Priest as he would leave this place-non-place sanctuary, would have conscious knowledge of this password and would reproduce it for the people. The multitude would then hear this "Explicit Name of God" and it would be immediately forgotten. This combined cognition and amnesia is certainly a hint to the idea of a password. After all, what is a password, if not something hidden and revealed at the same time?

If we put all this together we could come out with something like that: the cult of Yom Kippur, held before the monument to an Access Kit containing in itself the Absolute Program (the Torah), was the sending of a password. The major idea conveyed by this password was that the entire universe is ONE, this very here and this very place is where the earth and the heavens kiss. This place is all and any place, it is a portal. The people would than say "Praised be the Greatness of All", and would immediately fall to the earth in reverence as they took notice of such an impressive revelation.

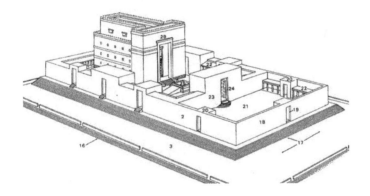

The Holy of Holies

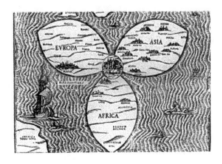

Jerusalem Axis Mundi

51

EXILE AND THE CONCEPT OF ABSOLUTE VIRTUALITY

Earlier, we talked about the efforts the rabbis made to prepare for the time of exile. Their greatest aim was to create virtual forms of keeping alive the beliefs and the cult of Israel. In addition to the Talmud and a praxis centering on time instead of space, exile itself contributed to the Jews' acceptance of the concept of a non-place. Eighteen centuries of wandering were strong enough to sink in this concept generating among Jews a great freedom from the attachment to a certain place. Unlike nomads, who had never internalized a sense of place, the descendants of Israel developed a duality of preserving the dream of return to a place, coming out of a deep experience of a non-place.

Many times this freedom from the attachment to a place and the mastery of the concept of non-place was treated with mistrust. Sometimes it even turned into hatred, as it interacted with a world where even the notion of nationhood was still embryonic. A world trying to consolidate itself in national loyalties had to live side by side with a people who functioned internationally, and who, annoying as it could have felt, were fundamental to the ruling powers, whose economies were very much dependent of international exchange. The Jews stood out both in commerce and finance, functioning within a network that has only recently been perceived and dealt with as part of our reality. They positioned themselves within society in a very strange place. They were not bounded by borders and felt very much at home dealing with others since they themselves were very much seen as the others.

This was certainly experienced as a threat and the Jews gradually turned into a dangerous and devilish kind of group. A world that did not know globalization, that protected itself within frontiers, came to project upon the wandering Jew its own fears. And the Jews turned out to represent a contagious group threatening the concept of nationhood. This precocity of the Jewish people in dealing with networks was so frightening that they were many times identified, despite their small numbers and insignificance in terms of real power, as a threat whose ultimate goal was to take over the world.

Rome, Byzantium, Spain/Portugal, England and France, and even contemporary Germany sought to conquer the world through colonization, the most concrete way of amassing power via the paradigm of place. The more places a nation controlled, the richer and more powerful it was. The Jews, prohibited for centuries from owning land, owning place, had a different modus operandi. They were a nation with no place; their colonialism had to do with non-place. They were seen as controllers of networks, and they engaged in commerce via the accesses of the planet's economic network. This is why, aside from other historical and religious factors, they evoked such fear and aggressiveness.

What is relevant here however, is the fact that the Jews became profoundly familiar with the dimension of non-place, or virtuality. Their economic activity was no more than a side effect of their basic approach to life. The nation of Israel's experience of virtualization became an important tool in its endeavor for survival and sustenance. But, again, that was merely an unfolding of a very deep perception of how things work in the broadest sense. On the depths of their experience Jews were developing a new paradigm of place. This was very clear from the perspective of a place oriented people to a very place detached people. Again, this might seem strange if we take in account that one of the main characteristic of the Jews was their longing for the return to the Promised Land. However, that was no other but just the surface of the survival skills Jews had developed. In a deeper level, their survival grew more and more dependent on the detachment from any place. Their return home was slowly transferred to the Messianic dream -- not that of the national return to Israel but the day when here will be felt like there, when every place will be home. This duality was clearly present at the creation of the State of Israel and is felt up to this very day. Theologically Jews were beginning to learn the advantages of virtuality over the so called reality and much of their cult was affected by that. The Yom Kippur as the central focal Festival is certainly an expression of this development. The old place -- Jerusalem/Temple -- was gradually substituted for a specific time. The archaic cult of portals came to be understood as a cult for the new paradigm of place, a cult for networks, for The Network. Saul An-Ski , a Russian 18th century dramatist, illustrates with precision this development into virtualization. In his play "The Dibbuk" he describes this profound transformation on the concept of places and centers:

"The world of G-d is holy, and among the holy lands of this world, the holiest is the land of Israel. In the land of Israel, the holiest city is Jerusalem. In Jerusalem, the holiest place was the Temple, and in the Temple the holiest place was the Holy of Holies.

There are seventy peoples in this world. Among these peoples there is the people of Israel. The holiest of the tribes of Israel is the tribe of Levi. Among the people of this tribe, the holiest are the priests. Among the priests, the holiest is the High Priest.

There are 345 days in the (lunar) year. Among these, the festivals are the holiest. Among these festivals the day of the Sabbath is the holiest. Among the Sabbaths, the day of Yom Kippur, the Sabbath of Sabbaths, is the holiest.

There are seventy languages in the world. Among them, the holiest is Hebrew. In Hebrew, nothing is more holy than the Torah. In the Torah, the holiest of all texts are the Ten

Commandments. Among the Ten Commandments, the holiest of all words is the Name of G-d.

All these holiest elements were brought together on the day of Kippur. In the holiest of holy places, the Sanctum Sanctorum; at the holiest of holy moments, Yom Kippur, the holiest of holy individuals, the High Priest, pronounced the holiest of holy words, the Divine Name.

Every place where a human being raises his eyes to the heavens is the Sanctum Sanctorum. Every human being, created in the image of the Creator, is a High Priest. Every day, every moment of a human being is a Yom Kippur. And every word uttered with perfect sincerity is the Name of G-d."

The discovery that every place is more than just a place was an intense experience of the Jewish people. Perhaps while Christians and Moslems concerned themselves with conquest of physical places, Jews by way of their exile were being provided with a sense of intimacy vis-à-vis the concept of non-place. Home, the Jewish hearth, came to be virtual. And in a world of impermanence, where every real structure is built by our minds, virtuality is quite efficient in so far as it responds to human experience.

The dreams of exile's end were in some way inspired by the recognition of this greater net ever present in every place that can be transcended. Exile's end will come when every individual is loyal to the net, understanding that he or she depends on being connected to it for survival. And if this loyalty was first oriented towards ones clan, moving then towards nation, and now, for the entire earth, we can conclude that it changed due to the evolutionary comprehension of the nature of the place we stand at. Human evolution could somehow be measured by the sophistication with which we locate ourselves within the network of reality.

It seems as no surprise the fame gained by the Hebrews of being a rebellious and an utopian people. Since Roman times the Hebrews came to represent a threat and a challenge to all forms of authoritarianism, for they could only operate with the idea that loyalty was owed solely to that which is absolute. Their commitment was not with any local reality but with that demanded by the Greater Net. The ethic or the act itself of not bowing to a minor authority or divinity, to no one but a sole and absolute G-d, is no more than a way of expressing a logic of non-place. This absolute place where we are is not a city, not a state, not a country, and not a planet. This place is immersed in interests far beyond such spheres. Recognizing these interests is much the same as recognizing the right of a nation to impose restrictions deriving from its own interests, on the interests of a state, which in turn would do the same to a city.

Understanding that we are citizens not of place --be it part of a nation or the world-- but that we are citizens of the universe in its most absolute dimension, means understanding ourselves as citizens of a non-place.

Saying this today is extremely dangerous, and out of context, words such as these can be treacherous. But all of those who have participated in twentieth century history know that we have committed unpardonable acts of betrayal, in the name of great loyalties. In protecting interests that are smaller than the larger ones we are capable to perceive, we become idolaters. Being a citizen of a place, namely failing to realize that a specific place is always a representation of all places, is an act of idolatry. Fascism and xenophobia were strong expressions of this kind of idolatry in this century. The truth is that we don't yet know the ultimate magnitude of our allegiance and in a reality as such in which we can't clearly define our rights and responsibilities, exile is the best citizenship. Artists, poets and intellectuals know this and are citizens of exile. In some way the tradition of the Hebrews recognized this through history and has turned much of that concept into theology.

After all, what are municipal, state and federal loyalties, if not windows to the same place? This ground I walk on, what place is this? From a very local point of view, it is as city. But this same place can open a window and perceive that the true interests of this place relate to its nature as part of a state. Or is this place a place relating to national or planetary interests?

Nazism, fascism and fundamentalism would all answer this question in different forms, all claiming that a place owes loyalty to the authority and power that conquers it. Tied to the paradigm of place, xenophobic Europeans and Americans, extremist Israeli colonists, Arab defenders of a holy war to liberate "places" are all the opposite of citizens of exile. They are citizens swallowed up by the ground, by place. If place is a door, it can lock and imprison just as well as it opens.

This feeling of being tied to a more concrete reality, to place, or the perception of the virtual dimension as a dangerous threat to humanity, is not only manifested by way of organized radical political movements. They are constant reactions that can be disguised variously, even by romanticism or humanism. This is because there is a dose of fundamentalism built into the individual who fears that human beings will become slaves to machines, or that media such as television or computers will harm the affective and intellectual spheres of human beings.

Every interactive process is a form of redemption from exile, of transformation of a place into this place. Interacting is the only way we have for avoiding our extinction, and it is a universal model; whatever interacts, survives. Our nascent discovery of ecology is just the start of an awakening to the dimension of oneness.

Interaction is the citizenship of exile. So-called virtual reality is not the reality of lies, the reality of what is not happening. What is virtual today is merely the representation of what does not yet possess a medium capable of making it perceived as absolute reality.

MYSTICAL CONSIDERATIONS
ABOUT MEDIA

This universe of which we are part is basically made up of filters. We cannot assimilate everything, all frequencies, and all the infinite nuances of this universe in the partial perceptions of our existence. To be who I am, I have to be a piece, a fragment, a differentiated element. Mystics from long ago thought of mysticism as a way to re-encounter the dimension of oneness, of non-differentiation. In Jewish tradition, we call this *d'vekut*, adhering (to oneness).

These filters are media. The computer and everything contained within it, television, radio, telephone, fax, etc., are filters allowing us to see beyond. They are not in themselves light, but instead, dark glasses allowing us to look at the light without being blinded. Think about it; media are like filters and veils over absolute reality, which paradoxically allow us to see more. In seeing less, we see and understand more.

Media produce forms of insensibility which, when we know how to use them, can broaden our awareness. They are limitations that can open doors to new dimensions of experience. This is a difficult concept.

When we reproduce the world in virtual form, and on the Internet, we are moving away from the real world while at the same time allowing ourselves greater comprehension of it. As we saw, primitive prayers worked like a net in exactly this way. Spending time inside a synagogue, a church, a mosque, or whatever special place for prayer, means being more distant from the concrete world; from the market, the street, from social interaction. This behavior can be terribly alienating, and spark a great deal of insensitivity, if it is not perceived as a medium, a veil, a limitation for seeing more. At the same time, such places as synagogues and churches are "servers" that can put us in direct connection with things that the market, the street, and social interaction cannot. This is because prayer, experienced as a medium, takes us to all markets, all streets, and all interaction. Its essence is virtual, and thus, pathless.

The idea of "pathlessness" is still new to us. What we understand of it today is but a small glimpse of what will come to be a definitive break with our archaic idea of place. And for Jews, this exile is far from ending at the creation of the State of Israel. Israel was a historic necessity and its value should not be underestimated, but much of its constitution is foreign to Judaism, not virtual enough for a people of exile.

The mystical expectation of the Jewish tradition focusing on the fortieth chapter of the Book Of Ezekiel paints a different future. This chapter, when Ezekiel describes a future Temple, allows an interpretation of Jewish tradition whereby the Third Temple will not be built. It will be brought from the heavens, built of fire, and offered by the Creator Himself.

Interestingly, this idea is present in contemporary visioning of the future. One of those is the "Academy of Jerusalem", an institution founded by Yitzhak I. Hayutman and dedicated to the reconstruction of the Temple. But how can this be done? Would it require leveling down the mosques located there today? No. According to their proposal it won't be there, but it will be there, it would be virtual. It will be immaterial, a central non-place for all peoples -- a non-place that will serve as a metaphor of all non-places.

If this project is the definitive project, we do not know for sure. What we do know is that there is something appearing on the horizon. We cannot see, only intuit.

In the words of Barbara Marx Hubbard, futurist follower of Teilhard de Chardin and Buckminster Fuller, "The New (celestial) Jerusalem is our collective potential for transcending all of creature's limitations, with the harmonious use of our abilities, achieving a society of human beings whose mind and bodies are a total reflection of the divine mind."

The Temple was always a medium. Perhaps the most primitive collective media invented by human beings were the concepts of gods, altars and temples. Interesting enough, temples were erected in the past and yet to this day we have not understood the reality for which the ancients built them. The "illumined" minds of our age ask: why was it necessary for the ancients to invest so much in such useless media. The answer is that they needed to, because the concept of virtual experience was always known to us. We came to learn of it through the consciousness of death. Death is the primary source of revelation when it comes to the comprehension of reality in life as something virtual and impermanent.

In this sense, life defined by the consciousness of death is also a kind of exile, one which helps us understand the virtual essence of everything.

MEANS AS END

Our understanding of any kind of discontinuity is sketchy. Intuition, for example, is a mystery to us exactly because it implies breaking with the logic of cause and effect. It is difficult and frightening to pass over an emptiness, over an unpaved area. The fear aroused by the experience of jumping over a pit without having any assurance that there is a steady ground to land at reveals much of the inherent limitations of our human structure. Deeply bound to the perception that the only dynamic element of our lives occurs in time, we want to measure results in terms of what will happen. Efficacy measured in time, however, is very tenuous. An old Chinese parable tells us:

"A sage owned a purebred horse and had a son. Everyone wanted to buy the horse from him, but he did not want to give up the animal. Some time later, the sage left the stable doors open, and the horse got out. His neighbors rushed to his house, saying, 'You should have sold the horse!' To which the sage replied, 'Maybe yes, maybe no." Some time later, the horse that ran away became the leader of a wild herd, and one day reappeared at the stables with another nineteen horses. The neighbors rushed to visit the sage once again, saying, 'you were right not to sell the horse!" He answered, 'Maybe yes, maybe no.' Not much later, the son of the sage was riding the horse, and he fell and broke his leg in four places. As a result, he became very ill and was bedridden for many months. The neighbors returned, saying, 'You see? If you had sold the horse, you would be better off.' The sage responded, 'Maybe yes, maybe no.' Not much later, a war erupted in the region. All the young men were drafted into combat and perished there. The saddened neighbors returned to the sage, saying, 'Yes... you did very well, not to sell your horse... To which the sage responded, with great conviction, 'Maybe yes, maybe no."

What will develop over time remaining is unknown to us. We easily identify victories and defeats that often reveal them to be, respectively, defeats and victories. All our anxiety lies in conquests, in getting somewhere, to an end. And what end is the end, the last end, if not the end? There is nothing in the future, except for windows and doors that it can offer to us, in the form of presents that will be constantly replaced. More than ever, we understand that not only do the ends not justify the means, but that they also do not justify themselves. The means, however, justify the ends. This is why the prophets of Israel were not so interested in predicting the end, the future, but in accessing the true present, the means.

A century ago, the activist and Jewish thinker *Achad Ha-am* wrote an ontological article titled, "Sacred and Profane". In it, he declared that in the dimension of the profane, the means derive their meaning from the end; when the end has been attained, the means automatically fall into disuse and disinterest. In the domain of the sacred, the end fills the means with meaning in and of themselves, such that, when the end has been attained, they do not lose their utility, but are redirected toward another aim.

According to him, profane books are nothing more than instruments to obtain knowledge of a particular subject matter. They are vessels of the ideas contained within them, and once they fulfill their role of informing, they fall into total oblivion. Thus it is with school texts which we never consult once we have gone through them. With sacred books, the opposite is true. In them, the content sanctifies the book, which gradually becomes the essence, while the content becomes ephemeral. The means is a non-place, unlike an end which is a place, arrived at or conquered. The place is profane. The non-place is sacred. In the latter, as with means, it is possible to redefine place, which is an end, as being any other place, any other end.

The sage in the Chinese parable, in answering, "Maybe yes, maybe no," is far from pathetic. For many, existence loses all flavors if it is not possible to define oneself as a success or a failure. Might our sage be depressed about being unable to control the world, unable to even distinguish the moments of greatness from those of misfortune? No. His way of getting beauty and pleasure from the world does not come from criteria based on the future, making it seem like a secure, established place. He lets himself go with the flow not of time, but of place.

Just as time has a there, a moment beyond, which we try to hack our way through to in our imaginations, or via the aging process itself, place has a future. The future of place is the dynamic that exists in the concept of place. The future of place is where this place takes me to another one. Although experience tells us we cannot be in two places at once (and we understand the world on this basis), a new paradigm is weakly revealing itself, whereby two different instants cannot occupy the same non-place. Non-place does not have time, does not know paths, and is made solely of doors and direct accesses. Through these one goes without going, because the aim is not to go, but to be, to be absolutely. A site on the net, a non-place, does not communicate by moving, but rather by being organically part of the rest, of any other site.

Once again, what is at stake here is the question of discontinuity. We understand how we will get to the future, since we can see a path paved with presents. Through fiction, we seek machines to take us from one time to another, instantly. We dream of teleporters that make us go from here to another place, without passing through anywhere else. Where did we get this strange intuition that this is possible? We most probably got it from the concept of place; from the very fact that a place can be many places.

An episode in Jewish history recounted in the Talmud sheds some light on this question. Rabi Hanina ben Tardion was a sage of Israel taken prisoner in Roman times, for passing on the teachings of his tradition. His punishment was cruel: being burned alive. To add to this cruelty, they wrapped his chest with damp parchment, so that his death would be slow. And to torture him even more, psychically, the parchment was nothing less than a scroll of the Torah, of the teachings the rabbi prized so well. In the face of this brutal scene, the daughter of the rabbi throws herself on the ground before her father, and asks, "Is this the Torah (law and justice) and is that its reward?"

The daughter's question is very pertinent. She is asking her father to make sense of what she perceives as reality. How can she put together the reality that her father is a good man whose life was dedicated to goodness and wisdom, with the reality of his being there, cruelly set on fire? The perception of reality does not fully take it in. Either the Torah -- that asserts a world controlled by the Creator -- is not real, or what is happening is not real. What is virtual? Understanding and human utopia, or his flesh and all that he is subjected to?

Rabi Hanina replies, "It is only the parchment that is burning, the letters (of the text) are being freed, and going directly to heaven." His daughter obviously was not concerned with the scroll of the Torah, wrapped around Rabi Hanina's chest. She is talking about the "Torah" as the way of life her father has led, and the "reward" doesn't have to do with the burning and desecration of the parchment, but with her father's physical integrity. Yet the answer works in both directions. Rabi Hanina is saying, "Daughter, it is my body that is being burned, the spirit -- the letters and text -- this goes to heaven." In other words, the situation fits into reality because what you are seeing is not what you are seeing. There is another way of seeing this place.

But the dialogue of father and daughter was interrupted by the executioner, and the Talmud tells us about it: "Master," said the executioner, "If I hasten your death, will you promise me eternal life?"

"I promise," said the old man. "Swear it," demanded the executioner. And Hanina swore thus. The executioner tore the parchment around Rabi Hanina, who delivered his soul to the Creator. The Roman soldier then jumped into the flames. A voice was heard from the heavens, proclaiming that Rabi Hanina and his executioner had entered jointly in the world to come. Rabi Yehudah wept on hearing this and made the following commentary, "Some people can achieve eternal life in a moment, while others need a whole lifetime."

Rabi Hanina's understanding of what is virtual was so clear and powerful that story is not finished until the executioner, the greatest symbol of what is concrete and real, gives himself over to it. As if the world were upside down, the victim shows mercy for his executioner. What's more, the executioner clearly sees that the fire is a portal. It doesn't matter that his character instantly turns from cruel (sadistically burning the sage) to just (being in the world to come, exactly like the sage Rabi Hanina). This is because that place turned into a portal. The executioner sees this and makes use of the doorway. Without it, his path would be long. The virtual world that Rabi Hanina revealed in the reply to his daughter provided the executioner with a medium.

The virtual world is an invitation to a voyage. It temporarily sets up a bridge with what we call reality, and makes it momentarily virtual. If an individual allows himself to move towards acknowledging the legitimacy of what was earlier virtual and turned into a portal, he passes through to the other side of it. When the door closes, when the place through which Hanina and his executioner access another place stops functioning as a portal, the "real" world returns to solidity. Nothing happened. The executioner went crazy with remorse, or something of the sort. Then we think, "What a silly end the two of them came to! They could have had another end." Finality, or what appears to be the end, is nothing more than a means. None of us can conceive the universe solely through its windows. All of us will have to go through portals, whether we wish to or not. Doors, the best means of all, are the heartbeat of the Creation. They are the greater connection between the point of the net we represent, and the web of encounters with all the rest.

QUANTUM ECOLOGY

As discussed earlier, a non-place is like a site. It is not a spatial place, but a door. When we discover, for example, the different relationships among living beings, i.e., an ecosystem, we are identifying doors. The way in which a given species affects our existence, or not, is a way to identify levels of interaction that exists among the different aspects of Creation. Ecological consciousness did no more than point to the fact that mosquito X or monkey Y has an open door that influences our destiny. There is something in them that interferes with us, and something in us that interferes with them. Little by little, we discover that we are in the same boat, and that what affects us affects others.

Reb Pinchas, a 19th century Chassidic leader, made some interesting comments when a disciple brought him the following question: "How can I pray, asking that someone repent his sins, when this prayer, if heard in heaven, clearly interferes in the free will of this person?"

The rabbi replied, "What is G-d? G-d is the very totality of all souls. Whatever exists as part of the total also exists as a part. Thus in every soul all souls are contained. If I change and grow as an individual, I contain in me the person I want to help, and he contains me in himself. My personal transformation helps to improve the 'he-in-me', and the 'me-in-him', also. In this way, it is much easier for the 'he-in-me' to improve."

If we analyze this hybrid language of spirituality and holography, we see that it assumes that in the internal world of each one of us, there is a connection with the other. The realization that this 'he-in-me' is a door, is just as astonishing as the perception that the 'me-in-him' is also a door from him to me. There is an ecology made up of interweaving, in which we have a little of each of all the others. We share many interweaving with human beings, with mammals, with living creatures, and even with minerals. These interweaving are the other in me. Our cells are impregnated with these interweaving. There are ameba dimensions in each one of us, or even reptile dimensions in each one of us.

This is what we want to save, when we talk about saving the whales or other species in extinction. In other words, we want to save the 'us-in-whales' in the name of the whales in us'. We are awakening bit by bit, as a generation, to say as Jacob did, "Certainly there is whale in this place (in me) and I knew it not." Or, "This (I) is no other place than the door to the whales". This "you-in-me", this interweaving of what we all are, means that we live much more collectively than we can imagine. Jacob's absolute perception was registered, when he declared, "This place is none other than the door to the heavens. Here, in this or another place out there, there is a G-d-in-me and a me-in-God. There is an absolute door to all and everything."

But if we cannot even perceive this yet, in relation to other human beings, with whom we have so many interweaving; imagine this with other species or all the rest of existence. It is part of human evolution to discover that the external world is a representation of place in each one of us. When we come to understand this, we will surprise ourselves with the recognition of how much our existence is a virtual representation of these countless interactions. Our lives are a means, a medium, a particular form of expression of these intricate interactions of the net.

The doors in us to others are a definition of ecology about the interior of our selves. The one-in-the-other is a cell, the ecological quantum. It is what allows us to open portals and access places. These do not occur in time or space, but through the other, into whom we can flow, if we know how to identify the him-in-us.

These are the secret passages of the castle of existence; knowing how to move through them is to be a voyager, a *netsurfer* through the interactions and links of this universe.

G-D IS THE PLACE

One of the names that Jewish tradition gives to G-d is ha-makom-- the place. In contrast, G-d is never called "time". Even though ancient sources utilize the concept of divine eternity, time is never presented as the key for greatest access to the Creator. G-d is neither in the past, nor the future. The Rabbi of Bratslav explains,

"G-d is above time. This is a truly frightening matter, one of the most incomprehensible of all. The human intellect cannot understand an idea such as this one. Know, however, that time is, in general, the fruit of ignorance; in other words, time seems real to us because our intellect is so small. The greater the intellect, the smaller is the significance of time. Look at dreams, for example. In dreaming, the intellect is asleep and all notion of time is transformed. In a dream, seventy years can go by in less than a quarter of an hour. There is a Mind so elevated that, for it, time represents nothing."

The Name of G-d, the Password above all others, of which we spoke earlier, is a word formed by four letters, a Tetragrammaton. This word, which cannot be pronounced, represents the contraction of all times by way of the combination of the letters of the words, past, present and future. This concept is often misunderstood. It does not mean, as we might think, that G-d is all time, and that His greatest attribute is eternity. The contraction of past, present and future express the disintegration of time, as the Rabbi of Bratslav implies. And where there is no time, we have the knot, the absolute contraction -- that which we are trying to identify as a non-place place.

A Biblical passage inspires a rabbinical commentary (*Or ha-Chaim*) which is quite relevant to the question of place. It is about the first verse of the book of Numbers: "G-d spoke to Moses in the Sinai desert, in the Tent-of-Appointment on the first day of the second month of the second year after their going out of Egypt."

The commentary asks a fairly banal question, "Why in the spatial dimension does the verse progress from the most generic element, to the more specific one, when with time the opposite is done? In space it is written --Sinai-- the more encompassing space, and then after, the Tent-of-Appointment; while with respect to time, there is a progression from the more specific --the day of the month-- to the more generic, the second year. In other words, wouldn't it be more logical to find a situation similar to the way we put our addresses on letters? First we have the name of the street, and then the name of the neighborhood or city.

The commentator's conclusion is that in reality, space is also presented going in the text from the more specific to the more generic. How? He explains.

"Our sages explained this by making use of another verse (Ex. 33:21): [G-d says:] 'Behold there is a place by me' (*hine makom iti*). This means that the 'Place' of G-d is built into G-d Himself (place by me). G-d is Place Itself in the world, but the world is not His Place. Thus, the Tent-of-Appointments, the locus where G-d was to be found, is the generic place of all the world, while the Sinai desert is nothing more than a specific location."

What the commentator wanted to point out is that the Place of G-d is not contained in a place. The point of access to a divinity, in this case the Tent-of-Appointments, is not less than nor is it part of the Sinai desert. On the contrary, it is this Tent that contains everything, including the Sinai desert.

Once again, we are talking about the meaning of the net. Many times people wonder about the Internet, where is its center? And of course, it is not easy to explain that there is no center of operations. The net exists, but it is in no place, or rather in all places.

Quite ancient commentaries look at the text mentioned above, in relation to Jacob's dream, intrigued by this story. The place of his dream is introduced by the strange expression, "and he lighted on a certain place". This is how the rabbis interpreted it (Gen. Rabah 68:9):

"Rabi Hunah said in the name of Rabi Ami, 'Why do we call the Eternal, The Place? We do it because He is the Place of the world.' Rabi Yosi said, 'We do not know if G-d is the Place of the world or if His world is his Place, but from the verse behold there is a place by me (the verse cited above), we conclude that G-d is the Place of this world, but this world is not His Place.'"

This seems to be Jacob's discovery: this place where I am is not the place of G-d, but G-d is this place. His dream was in fact great evidence of this. Jacob dreams of angels who ascend and descend a ladder reaching the heavens. This G-d that is, but is not in the place, is in Himself the non-place, the net itself. The center of the net is G-d. Thou shall not make images is the recommendation of a tradition that knows that G-d is not a form, nor even an entity, but the active-inter-active process of everything.

As we said earlier, Jacob witnesses an access. What is this ladder, if not the great net that goes from this world to the heavens? The sages were intrigued with these angels that "ascend and descend" the ladder. They asked, "In dealing with angels... might they not be 'descending and ascending', instead of 'ascending and descending'? The answer lies in the fact that the angels are connectors, an archaic representation of what a message and direct communication with the net are.

The etymology of the word "angel" (*malach*) is in fact, "messenger". These messengers are agents present in any everyday situation when we make contact and we connect ourselves. Intuition, synchronicity, and other experiences often visualized by way of angels are in fact direct accesses to the net. Jacob witnesses a moment of connection. His angels ascending and descending are the bytes sent and the bytes received in any contact with the net. Using these, Jacob could download information from this Absolute Net, and this astonished him.

G-d is the place. Rather, G-d is the non-place in any place.

PART IV

WHERE VIRTUALITY
AND REALITY
KISS

THE LITERALITY OF METAPHOR

The main aim of this book is to think about a new metaphor provided to us by the Internet. We could say that the metaphor in question is the whole ultra-modern process of communication and multimedia. But the Internet is the most sophisticated concrete communication tool we have, to widen our horizons and create a language for talking about what in the past was only accessible to intuition.

The rabbis have always been interested in metaphors and how they enlighten understanding. A story about the rabbi of Saragossa illustrates this. The rabbi said:

"We can always learn something about everything that exists in this world!

--What can we learn about a train, for example? a disciple challenged him.

--That because of a second, we can lose everything.

--And a telegraph?

--That every word is counted and we will be charged for it.

--And the telephone?

-- That what we say here is heard there."

We realize that all communication media can be used as metaphors for a great network. That the Windows program and the Internet can serve as tools for talking about the net. In this case, even the language that these innovations have brought, greatly reflect the metaphor they build.

Virtuality, like the theory of relativity, shows us that frontiers are not about internal or external order. Frontiers are in the mind, and its ability to perceive, or in the media that frame sensibility. G-d is not in a place, nor in any time, but in the possibility of using the mind to see. And it is exactly at the times when we perceive the limits of our minds, that we become apprehensive about concepts such as virtuality.

We fear that people will lose contact with reality, that they will isolate themselves with computers or any other means that may come to be invented. We fear people will become more distant, that real experience will be replaced with virtual existence. That we may come to hear, see, taste, smell and touch a world that is not real.

Science fiction can no longer imagine the future because it recognizes that this implies radical breaks with our current comprehension. Seeing that the new technology brings constructive progress is difficult, because it is threatening to our understanding of the world.

When the telephone was invented, people imagined that the world would be a place of fewer personal encounters. When television arose, we worried that it would turn viewers into one dumb mass. The concern is justified. The poor use of anything is worrisome. But we must distinguish our fear of excess from the notion that virtuality means replaces the great marvels of so-called reality. Eating, dancing, loving and so many other activities of reality won't be abolished by the development of ever-more virtual processes. The world will find its equilibrium, because it will need to.

Notably, a forgotten aspect of this discussion is the fact that everything we label as "real experiences" are in fact virtual.

Things cannot be seen, without the medium of eyes. There is no odor, taste or sound that is not a virtual production of our sensory media. Even touch, so "real" that it is the cry for help of those that dream -- pinch me-- is the product of sensory media made of nervous systems and neurons. The Psalms (135) proclaim, "They have mouths but they speak not; they have eyes but they see not..." We are virtual.

The greatest proof of this is death. Lacking the means, the media to express ourselves, we come to be entities that are no longer part of "reality". We say someone has gone, and we deal with that reality without questioning it, although no one knows where he or she went. What we understand from the perspective of life is that we have lost contact with that expression known as so-and-so. We weep a great deal over death, because we think we have forever lost contact with our dead.

What we know as reality will not be substituted by the virtuality of the Internet or of any other instrument of the future. But the metaphor of these innovations will help us to understand life and existence itself, in a way that is very different from today's way of thinking. Knowing how to absorb all the teaching contained in metaphors, making them part of the real world, making them literal, is an art we must all develop.

An episode that took place 2,000 years ago is worth mentioning here. It is about a visit the sages made to the non-place. The Talmud tells us:

"Thus taught the sages: Four sages entered the orchard of secret knowledge. They were Ben-Azai, Ben-Zoma, Elisha, and Akiba. Akiba warned the others, 'When we come near the place where the marble pillars are, or when we are sunk in the immensity of whiteness, do not cry --Water! Water! -- as this will be a lie, and no liar can stand before G-d.'

Because they did not follow his instructions, Rabi Akiba's companions were punished. Ben-Azai looked, and died. Ben-Zuma looked, and went mad. Elisha looked, and lost his faith. Only Rabi Akiba entered in peace and left in peace."

This story is an amazing description of the manner in which the gates to the net, the orchard, were known in the past. Such is the Talmud's clarity that it tells us that this orchard is a virtual world. We know that the world "orchard" in Hebrew, *pardes*, is made up of the initials of four words: literal, metaphor, allusion and secret. These four dimensions of interpretation that the human mind recognizes does not grant exclusivity to the literal world, as a representation of reality. These dimensions of the mind are virtual. The world the sages enter is not a place, nor a moment in time. The sages enter the network. The great danger lying therein is not knowing how to find ways to bring this virtual experience back into the realm of experience. Not knowing how to digest what is shown them is what causes so much destruction among the first three sages.

Rabi Akiba had warned against trying to turn this virtual world, a non-place, into a place. He alerted them against thinking that what looks like water is water. In doing this, "you will be lying", he warned. But the sages saw, and tried to make sense of the virtual. They got lost in the orchard. Ben-Azai dies because not "knowing where one steps" is potentially lethal. Ben-Zuma goes mad because he could not overlay the countless realities of one place, into his limited mind. Elisha, in a superhuman effort, managed to integrate everything he saw, but his limitations made him understand it in a distorted manner. Only Akiba could enter and leave the orchard. He did this because he deeply understood what a door is, what an access is, and what a net is.

BACK IS FRONT

Some of civilization's most important symbols seek to represent this archaic perception that humans had long ago concerning the interweaving that exists in a given place. Jacob's visualization is present in the Star of David, in the Yin/Yang and the Cross. The first is two interlocking triangles, one pointing to the process that funnels from above to below, the other funneling from below to above. The place it accesses, symbolized by the triangle converging on a point above, meets with the net it provides access to, symbolized by the triangle converging on a point below.

The Yin-Yang too, with its oriental "rounded" peculiarities, has a white dot in the middle of a black space, and a black dot in the middle of a white space. This dot that crosses from one reality (white or black) into another, is the door that makes the white have access to the black, and vice-versa. The black is the place of the white, and the white is the place of the black. Everything is included in everything. The Cross, in the other hand, marks a site in the same way that mathematics marks a point. The meeting point is not part of the horizontal or the vertical dimension, but of both at the same time. It is the knot of heaven and earth.

One Biblical episode deals incisively with this question of the distinction between reality and virtuality. It is the text of the last verses of Exodus 33. This text, mentioned earlier, recounts a dialogue between G-d and Moses. Moses asks G-d to tell him more about the essence of reality and of his plans. Moses says to G-d (33:12):

> "See, thou sayest unto me, Bring up this people: and thou hast not let me know whom thou wilt send with me. Yet thou hast said, I know thee by name and thou hast also found grace in my sight. Now therefore, I pray thee, if I have found grace in thy sight, show me now thy way, that I may know thee..."

Moses wants to know the way, and to know G-d. His plea for more power of understanding, for a more absolute comprehension of reality, is astonishing, coming from a man such as Moses, with whom G-d, according to the text (33:11) spoke "face to face". Moses is even more explicit (33:18), and says to G-d, "I beseech thee, show me thy glory." G-d then replies, "I will make all my goodness pass before thee, and I will proclaim the name of the Lord before thee...thou canst not see my face, for there shall no man see me, and live... (However) Behold there is a place in me... and while my glory passeth by,... I will cover thee with my hand while I pass by: And I will take away mine hand, and thou shalt see my back parts, but my face shall not be seen."

Moses wants to see reality as something concrete. He wants to know "glory", face to face. G-d then has to explain to him that no human being can see his face and live. It is perhaps this attempt that takes away Ben Azai's life when he enters the orchard. It is impossible to conceive this absolute reality, by way of the media that we humans are. But if it is not possible to be G-d and contain in oneself His reality, we can at least take in the meaning of the words "behold a place by me". You can access me, G-d explains. Moses' eyes are then covered by a filter (the hand of G-d), so as not to be blinded. This medium symbolized by the hand of G-d is what allows a view of His back-- reality in virtual form.

The face of G-d which Moses could access was not the true face. This, he could not see and go on living. What he thought was the face was in fact G-d's back. This is because all reality for human beings, as we said earlier, is a virtual expression of true reality. G-d even mentions explicitly the means, the media, used to virtually access his "glory". What are they? I will make all my goodness pass before thee, and I will proclaim the name of the Lord before thee. Passing all His goodness before a human being means activating his gratitude, which in itself is a great medium through which we perceive the existence of the Creator and we praise Him. To proclaim the Name of G-d is symbolic of the "password" needed to perceive the universal net to which this Name gives access.

Our humanity leads us to think the back is the front. Reality is not a face, but a back. Thus, we cannot presume too much about this new dimension of the metaphor we call virtuality. We cannot, being who we are, reduce everything to the realm of the literal and the real. If we are to at least see the back, we will have to learn to accept that which will only come to us by the way of the virtual.

DOWNLOAD IN HISTORY

The history of the Hebrews is especially interesting when it comes to the divine Revelation. Of all the possible spiritual concepts the Hebrews could have come up with, they opted for one in particular: the Creator, in some moment of History, would pass on information to his creations. The reception of the Tablets of Law on Mount Sinai is a sophisticated and original understanding of the net and its media, that make up the universe.

Lets take a look at the story in its great wealth of detail. Moses is called to the top of the mountain to receive the Creator's software. It is as if G'd were saying, "Look here, Moses, here is a basic program for you to give to the humans. It is a program for running any other program. Make it sacred by giving copies to everyone. Read them publicly, in a ritual. Its structure is binary --'do' and 'do not'."

These were the Ten Commandments, or as we call them today, the *mitzvot* (commands).

The content of the information the Creator would pass to his creations went from a very sophisticated means, or medium (the absolute medium), to one that was infinitely inferior. This was as if the download (the passage of information from one medium to another, from one terminal to another) was from a medium infinitely superior to a Pentium, to another, infinitely inferior to an AX. In the synagogue, every time the public reading of the Torah is finished, we declare, "This is the Torah that Moses presented to the people of Israel, from the mouth of G-d, by the hands of Moses (Num. 9:23)!" By the mouth of G-d" is the means by which the information is issued; "by the hands of Moses" is the receiving medium.

Try to imagine the difficulty of passing information from one incredibly sophisticated medium, to an incredibly obsolete one. The Creator would have had to use fantastic filters, to reduce Himself to the capacity level of the "hands of Moses". If the Creator had not passed the information in human language, the Revelation would be incomprehensible, both for Moses and the people. There would be strange symbols, like those covering our computer screens when we cannot read a particular document. The work of later generations up to our times and through all human history, has been to rescue the original meaning of the Revelation, of what, beyond the filters, was being sent from the net to an access point. According to Kabbalistic tradition, two different fires print this program, one white, the other black. One is the "real" text before us until our days, the other is the "virtual" text that awaits metaphoric interpretation, allusive and secret, to rescue the true meaning of the Revelation.

What the divine representation of the net expects of human beings is then translated into concepts intelligible to our obsolete AX, such as : thou shalt keep the Sabbath... thou shalt not steal... thou shalt not kill... thou shalt not covet, and so on. But the remnants of the volume and density of the information that arrived and was converted into information that humans could understand is registered in a Hebrew legend. It tell us that G-d began to "recite" the Commandments and that at the first letter of the first uttered word, the people begged Moses to intermediate the reception of the Torah. What was this letter? The letter "alef", a silent letter. This silence brought with it such intensity of information, that the people fell with their faces to the ground, in fear of this transmission. If the silent letter conveyed so much intensity, we can't even imagine what the "sounding" of the other letters that had a pronunciation would bring about. Moses had to be turned into an intermediary, a "service provider" so that the information could reach the common human being.

The first recommendation of this master program called the Torah (1.0) was about the oneness of the Creator (of the net)-- "I am YHWH (the Tetragrammaton password) your G-d." The first recommendation was keep "realities" distinct. "Thou shalt not have other gods before me... thou shalt not make representations or images of what is above in the heavens..." is a warning not about the dangers of virtuality, but the dangers of "reality". To attribute absoluteness to any "reality" is an unpardonable error, fruit only of an insensibility of equal absoluteness.

In all this, it is fundamental to understand that the metaphors the Hebrews passed on to us are totally in tune with the mechanics of a net in operation. There is a net-universe and the downloading of information from it is possible. The parallel works to such an extent that even G-d speaks of this program downloaded to humans, using the following words (Deut. 30:11):

"For this commandment which I command thee this day, it is not hidden from thee, neither is it far off. It is not in heaven, that thou shouldest say, Who shall go up for us to heaven, and bring it unto us, that we may hear it, and do it?... but the word is very nigh unto thee, in thy mouth, and in thy heart, that thou mayest do it." G-d defines here the non-place. Thou needest not seek nothing in hidden places, or in places of any sort. Here, in your heart, in the place, all this is accessible. You don't have to travel far, not even move from your place, if you have access.

The Revelation in history is a collective episode of what every individual can experience by way of his own doors. We must not search in the external worlds, in illusory "realities", what can be accessed virtually within our own selves.

VIRTUALITY AND MESSIANISM

Just as our generation is fascinated by science fiction, there was also great interest in times past, in the discoveries to be made in the future. But there was a difference. Our science-permeated culture trusts to science itself, to attain the marvels of the future. We believe that the means themselves will be the great gift of the future, while the ancients thought of them as mere metaphors paving the way to the world of the future.

The ancient world wisely realized that pleasure and human happiness do not increase with the use of scientific gadgets or any sort of discovery. If we could go from New York to Boston in five minutes, or if we had 3D television at home with 500 entertainment channels, we would not necessarily be happier. Happiness is a form of equilibrium with life that does not depend on the applications it offers us. Even if the greatest promise of science were to increase the human lifespan, or to provide immortality, these possibilities make no sense until we know the reason for life itself.

For one to be immortal not dying is not enough; there must be a deep understanding of why one should not die. In fact, we haven't the slightest idea of what is necessary, beyond the mere fact of not dying, for attaining immortality. In other words, life is also limited by what we are able to see.

But Jewish tradition had two fictional ideas relating to immortality, which were incorporated into western civilization. The first was the idea of the Messiah; and the second, the resurrection of the dead.

Messianic belief was an intuitive construct claiming that one day, an understanding of the world would be definitively installed, that would neutralize humanity's greatest enemy. And who was the greatest enemy? The very human being himself! The greatest and most unacceptable violence in our history has been perpetrated by human beings. The cruelty of this violence was more lethal than any natural disaster. The memories of the injustices and betrayals of the past are more intensely painful than the pain of past disease. Harmony among human beings implies ending the predatory desire for prosperity and the feeling of envy, or at least bringing these to insignificant levels. Such an event would have a tremendous impact on the planet and our quality of life.

But how could this be possible? Not through advances in reality, but advances in virtuality. This world can be transformed, not by way of any external discovery, but by an internal one. All the external world can do for us is to provide metaphors to wake us out of our torpor. Deep changes in the perception of life and its priorities will demand a radical re-reading of reality.

Hebrew tradition expresses in one of its most important prayers* this hope, that one day the world will be populated by beings who understand that reality is nothing more than a portal to other realities:

"On us (who see virtually) lies the responsibility of transmitting the grandiosity of the Creator (of the net), since He did not make us as the masses who bow to lesser realities... We hope, thus, that all humanity may very soon be able to call Your Name and accept your sovereignty over it (which we perceive as virtual) ... And on this day YHWH will be absolute in all the universe, on this day YHWH will be One and His Name will be One."

The ancient world intuited that one day a tremendous insight will occur, whereby all humans will have access to a door. Through it will come universal consciousness of the

---

* **Aleinu** Leshabeach, the traditional Sidur

existence and reality of the oldest collective virtual concept of civilization-- the Creator.

This new term, virtuality, has come to offer us another choice between the only two qualifications that were at our disposal: real and illusion. Freud, in his most open criticism of religious tradition, wrote a book entitled "The Future of an Illusion". Perhaps he was predicting with this title the idea that many of our contemporary "illusions", that certainly can foment many forms of pathologies, are mixed up in the deepest part of our unconscious, together with primeval intuitions and memories. Ironically in relation to the content of the book, we could make a play in words and derive from this title the concept that the nature of "illusions" is evolutionary, or transformational. Because there is a future to "illusions", they will not be as they are perceived today. The future of "illusion" is the fact that this concept may transcend the domain of "lies" and become virtual. Our unsophisticated senses cannot perceive it, but our more sensitive capabilities have access to a dimension of reality very much present in that which is commonly understood as illusion.

The technology of dealing with the virtual is very old. While today we have access to virtuality using our computers' visual and communication capacities, the past had its own "instruments" for penetrating this dimension. Media, as noted earlier, was text. This is the exercise the four sages were engaging in, when they entered the orchard. It is this entry and departure, when both undertaken in peace, that symbolized the Kabbalist's journey through unreal worlds. Journeys to the virtual world accessed through text are one of the most effective ways to transcend the limits of our senses and our mind.

An example of this journey, limited by what we can comprehend from means as poor as a book, is the commentary by Rabbi Schneersohn, the last Lubavitch rabbi.* The rabbi

---

* This commentary was told to Reb Zalman Schachter, who heard it from the rabbi himself in a house of study in France, at the end of World War II.

connects two Talmud texts, turning them into a portal to obtain virtual information. The first is a dry, technical text on the appropriate day for a wedding. It says, "A virgin marries on the fourth day, a widow on the fifth, and a divorced woman on the sixth..."

The other text says, "Before the eyes of G-d, a thousand years is like a day." On a superficial level, the first text is quite banal. A virgin married on the fourth day*, because the morning of the fifth day was when the rabbinical tribunal met to judge small claims. Among these claims might be a complaint from a bridegroom who discovered on his wedding night that his wife was not a virgin. Thus it was convenient to marry on the fourth day, since on the following day the marriage could be undone at the request of the groom, if the bride was not a virgin.

But the rabbi took this text out of its "real" context, and put "filters" on it to transcend not only the noises of time and old-fashioned customs, but its focus as well. He realized that the word marriage is also a metaphor for the connection among human beings and the Creator. According to Jewish tradition, The Revelation on Mount Sinai was a linkup between the Creator and his creation. In fact, a marriage certificate-- the Torah-- was conferred on those involved in the event. And this makes a great deal of sense in the ancient world, where love was the best known invisible (virtual) "connection" of daily life. The love of G-d provided this "coupling". Note that the verb to know in Hebrew has the same root as the verb to penetrate**, and is used many times to describe sexual relations.

In Jewish tradition, there are three requirements for a wedding: a canopy, where the ceremony takes place, a marriage certificate, and the sexual act. If one of these is absent, there

---

* **Mondays and Thursdays** were market and public events day.
** **penetrate** - Andre Chouraqui, translates the verb *ladaat*, which means both *know* and *penetrate*. "Adam knew Eve" is a description of their first sexual act. Penetrating a woman is getting access to a place in the most literal sense.

is no marriage. The document had been given to the Hebrews in the form of the Torah; the ceremony under the canopy was celebrated at Sinai. All that is missing to make this marriage a binding one is the "coupling". When is this to happen? When will this ultimate intercourse take place, filling all creatures with a fertile flow of information and awareness?

Here is where the second text comes in. If, for the Creator "a thousand years is like one day", when will the wedding take place? We return to the first text. "A virgin is married on the fourth day, a widow on the fifth day, and a divorced woman on the sixth day." If every day is "like a thousand years" for the Creator, the marriage should have taken place in the fourth millennium.

Notably, the Jewish calendar registers this year as the 5758th after the creation of the world. Thus, more than 1,800 years ago, this marriage should have taken place. This is when a great deal of Messianic activity took place, in Israel at the time of Jesus. But why didn't it happen? It didn't happen because Israel was no longer a virgin. The symbol of a people who commit adultery and betray their commitment to the Creator is widespread in Jewish theology. If Israel cannot marry on the fourth day as a virgin, what day can the wedding take place? Certainly not on the fifth day, since Israel is not a widow (as Nietzsche has proposed). She is divorced. Yes, since the idea of adultery implies a divorce from the lesser gods she espoused, so as to be able to contract the long-awaited marriage. If Israel is divorced, when will the wedding be? It will take place on the sixth day, namely, the sixth millennium.

If we are in the year 5758, this is already the sixth millennium, with only 242 years to the end, and the start of the seventh millennium. The wedding approaches. The rabbi said it was closer than most people thought. If the wedding is on the sixth day and this is the eve of the Sabbath, this means that for Jews there are still other restrictions. A wedding cannot take place on the Sabbath, and as this begins not at midnight on Friday, but at sundown, and the Sabbath rules go into effect one hour before sundown, then the wedding must be about to take place.

This is an example of the kind of work that goes on in virtual space. Reality is marked by the reality of text. We can ask ourselves if this same reality speaks the truth. When human beings collectively perceive the logic and the metaphors of the virtual world, these can become more legitimate truths than the status quo of so-called concrete reality.

The Messianic era is in our heads, ready and conceived. It is a deep objective of any human being, to turn the virtual into the real.

PART V

THE LAST FRONTIER
OF VIRTUALITY

THE RESSURECTION OF THE DEAD

Of all the virtual scenarios that humans can create in their dreams and imaginations, the most daring of all is to conquer death. Once again, our world can only think in terms of reality. Scientific efficiency always centers on control. Thus, the only way to beat death is through immortality. Death is seen as an adversary, as if it were a disease.

The virtual world offers an alternative: death can be a door. It must not be conceived necessarily as a locked door, but rather serve as a way for access.

This strange idea of resurrecting the death is probably the outcome of deep meditations in Jewish tradition on the outrageous possibilities that the future can bring about. Or better, the possibilities that the future can make available to us through access, since everything the future will bring about already exists now. All that we lack in the present is access . In reality this idea of "resurrection of the dead" has never been fully clarified, even within Jewish tradition itself. Maimonides tried to give it some meaning, once this idea became central to Jewish theology, but his explanations do not clear everything up. Apparently, at a given moment, all those who have lived will be revived. But no one can explain when and how they will live. Will they then be immortal? Will those who are still alive at that moment also be raised to the category of immortals? And how will the world then be?

This concept does not lie outside of mainstream Jewish thinking. Unlike other doctrines, such as reincarnation, the resurrection of the dead is a normative concept of Judaism, and is even part of the liturgy of daily prayer. Why would there be so little information about such a central idea?

Studying this theme gives the impression that the rabbis could not explain what this concept meant, using words. They knew that conquering death belonged not to the human sphere, but to the divine one. At the same time, if we cast aside the notion of reality as dictated by science, it might be possible to forge a new understanding of death that would not see it as a kind of break or discontinuity. The rabbis understood that being in touch with another person that is alive, and then experiencing him suddenly disappear by the way of death, is a limitation of our media as humans. When this media can contemplate the world aided by other media, or perhaps by way of sensibilities that are now idle aspects of our media, death can be a door. Again, by door they meant the establishment of borders and instances, which at the same time make it possible to imagine that we can pass through it and even return through it.

I suggest that the fundamental idea expressed by the resurrection of the dead is that there will be a crowning event, whereby the frontiers will be understood as doors. They are experienced as doors today-- there are those who die and those who are born-- but they are not fully comprehended as such. The possibility of entering death virtually, of communicating more directly with the net and through it, accessing the non-physical dimension, will be experienced as a resurrection of those who have already died. They will not be brought back to life, but we will access them and that which was experienced as a discontinuity will be linked to life in a conscious way. It is important to understand though that this is not a matter of talking with the dead, as if they were in another world, as several spiritualist traditions have. It is not a communication with the dead but an access to the network where even the dead take part.

And if they are a part they can then be brought to the status of resurrected. They become linked and not deleted.

What will bring this incredible revolution is another medium. Three hundred years ago, if someone said it would be possible for people in Brazil and Japan to speak to each other instantaneously, people would have imagined shouting very loudly. Fifty years ago, no one would have imagined that this would be possible without a line. Today, through the air, I talk with people in Japan. Just as today, I can share speech and vision with Japan, one day my hand will go instantly to Japan, and shake a partner's hand. This place will be that one, and that one will be this.

In the interpretation we saw above, by the Rabbi of Lubavitch, the world will become Messianic in the virtualization of our relation with the world. Our interests will no longer lie with people and places, but with everyone and everything. On that day, there will be a globalization of all interests, not just economic affairs. A thousand years after the start of this process of peace and harmony, at the end of the seventh millennium, on the week end, the divine *shabbat*, another week will begin. But at the end of this Sabbath of millennia, we will know the resurrection of the dead. This will be a chance to dive into the net that, if organized by some sensitive media, can allow us to virtually touch every creature that ever lived on earth.

The rabbis are wise to keep quiet about this event. Every attempt to make it more explicit will result in fiction that can easily fall prey of our own desires, fantasies and wishful thinking. Yet we must recognize the validity of a certain intuition that all worlds, whatever they are, meet in a non-place. Once more, it is important to note the difference between interweaving with a non-place and interweaving with a place. This is the very difference between evoking the dead and having access to that which they are still part of. The attempt to force these different worlds, separated by doors, into a place is a transgression of the limits of our sensory media, and mixes up virtuality and illusion. Non-place is the space of these events. They will be virtual, just as everything is.

103

ELIJAH,
CHAIRS, WINDOWS AND DOORS

If we are on the subject of virtuality and death, the legendary figure of the prophet Elijah cannot be left out. This is because Elijah did not die, but also is not alive. The Bible story tells of his "exit" from this world as ascension to the heavens in a cyclone". The prophet himself repeatedly guaranteed to Elisha, his greatest disciple, that "As the Eternal lives and as you live... I will not depart from thee." Based on this affirmation, Jewish popular tradition and folklore developed a unique relationship with the presence-non-presence of Elijah. He is always present at important events of the Jewish rituals dealing with the life cycle. At circumcision, for example, a chair is left for Elijah. At Passover, a chair and a wineglass are placed for him, and the ceremony includes the ritual door-opening in every home where the feast is commemorated, to receive the prophet.

Jewish tradition created a very strange way of honoring the singularity of this character, he who is there, but not there.

Jewish folklore was even more creative. Elijah appears and disappears at the most unlikely times and places. He can be seen in the market, manifesting himself in an interface with the more mundane and concrete world. Or, he can dress up as a beggar and surprise people, able to appear not only in any place or at any moment, but also in any form or as any entity. He is in general a wandering figure, an unburied person who is totally at ease with his situation. Unlike a troubled soul, he wanders thought the worlds in great happiness. And to make his archetype even more mysterious, tradition gives him the task of announcing the start of the Messianic era, and the arrival of the Messiah.

His character is truly intriguing. But why so much deference and what exactly does he represent, symbolically?

Elijah is not an immortal, and thus, of no divine order. He is mortal, and proof of this is his resignation of his earthly life exemplified by having passed on to his disciple Elisha the task of continuing his work. In other words, Elijah dies, just like Moses, the man who spoke with G-d face to face. Yet Elijah is a model entity, a prototype of the human beings who will inhabit the world he will one day come to announce. A moment will come in history, when human beings will be bathed in divine inspiration (prophecy), and will become as sensitive as Elijah. Because of his sensitivity, Elijah is able to beat back death. This occurs not because he is immortal, but because he is timeless.

By timeless, we mean not temporary or interim, but above all capable of transcending our mundane and primitive comprehension of time. An immortal controls death and is divine. But someone who is timeless is not in time, exists in a virtual sense, and makes himself present by way of the net of which he is part.

Elijah is not real, because to be real he would have to be alive. Elijah is also not dead, since if he were, he would be an illusion. Elijah is a presence because he is virtual. Above all, he represents someone who has access to door and windows. He can promise to always be present and can fulfill his promise.

A passage from the Kabbalist Iossef Caro does much to clarify the symbolism of the Elijah archetype. He recommended: (*The Way of the Mystics*)

"When you want Elijah to become visible before you, concentrate yourself on him before going to sleep. There are three ways to perceive him: in your dream,... while awake and able to greet him, ... while awake and able to greet him and have this greeted returned."

These are three ways to be in a non-place. The first is the most concrete form of not-being in a place. This is about imagination and dreams. In this non-place which is so much a part of daily life (to which we give names and deal with in a concrete manner), we are so good at fooling the media of our sense, that we can actually taste virtuality. But it appears to us as an illusion. Imprisoned inside our concrete reality, we cannot legitimate this play world, cannot call it true. On this level, Elijah is just a symbolic chair static and imprisoned in the home built by our objective senses.

We can, however, go farther. We can transcend the dimension of our home through its windows. These can take us not only to dream or conceive the presence of Elijah, but to truly see his reality. From the window, he greets us, symbolizing the interference of another reality, making itself perceptible.

But in the deepest sense, we can go beyond being affected by this reality external to our own, and actually penetrate it. To perceive Elijah and relate to him outside of reality, where a neither-dead-nor-living-person greets us and we can return the compliment, is to go beyond the limits set out by doors.

The house we build of chairs, windows and doors is made to protect us. It protects us from the sun, the rain, the wind and even from other people. Yet it is exactly from all these that we derive our survival. What would be of us without sun, rain, wind, and other people? We protect ourselves from what we most need, from what feeds the very viability of our existence. Thus it is with reality. We protect ourselves from reality by way of senses that limit, that cover up the intensity of what we most need.

Elijah rose to the heavens, and by giving himself over to the net without making use of the metaphor of disconnection, of death, he became the archetype of connection to the net. This

Nilton Bonder

Elijah in any place, at any moment or in any form, is everything contained in everyone. He is the greatest example of what is at home, not being at home. He is the master who understood that exile in its most profound sense is being truly at home. And this is what he will bring to us, as "good tidings".

THE PROMISED LAND--PLACE

If there is something the Hebrew tradition left us as a metaphor, it is that of the Promised Land. The promise remains to this day, and the exile of the Jews is not solely defined by their separation from the land of Israel. This people have been exile ever since Biblical times, seeking their land, never finding it. Once settled, something is missing from its identity as the Promised Land.

When the Bible tells us of Moses sending spies to bring news of this "promised place", they return with a report mixed with fear and awe. They say, (Num 13:27,32, 33) "We came unto the land whither thou sentest us, and surely it flowerth with milk and honey... The land through which we have gone to search it, is a land that eateth up those who settle in it; and all the people that we saw in it are men of a great stature. And there we saw the giants, the sons of Anak, which come of the giants: and we were in our own sight as grasshoppers, and so we were in their sight."

The Zohar, the greatest written reference source on Jewish mysticism, understands this story as if the spies had really seen such fantastic things. They were in the Promised Land, and the reality of this land unfolded itself into many. They are realities that can take on frightening form, but above all, this place "eateth up those who settle in it".

According to Chassidic interpretations, this land "eats" in two ways. For some people, it is dangerous because it is the settling in the place that devours them. These people can only see a more immediate and concrete reality. Routine, sustenance taken from the earth, consumes them. They cannot see anything of a density less than that of land. Everything must be hard, heavy, and reproducible as an experience, in order to be real. These people inhabit, or better, they are slaves, of the dimension of place. For them this Promised Land is very dangerous for they cannot grasp its real essence as a non-place. They became depressed and despair consumes them.

The second group is made of those that react in the opposite direction. They can lose themselves completely in the marvels and illusions that come from a non-place. Seduced either by the pleasure (milk and honey) or by the suffering and terror (giants) that emanates from this non-place they see a door that provides access turn into a door that leaves them locked outside. Nothing of a more solid nature, such as land, appears to attract or satisfy such people. All they can relate to is on the way of virtuality and there is no safe return to the experience of reality. The result is that they go mad, or become heretics.

There is virtuality about this Promised Land, that prevents it from being a place. As such , as an orchard, it poses tremendous dangers to those who do not know how to inhabit it without being swallowed up by it. Rabi Akiba would certainly be a good citizen of this land. This land is virtual, and has to be understood from the perspective of a net reaching out toward a site. The spies said they felt like grasshoppers in the giants' eyes. How did they know what the giants saw? They knew because this is the land where the perspective is not from one to all, but from all to one. There, they do not find giants, but the Other, G-d. In Isaiah (40:22), it is asked, "Who is he that sitteth upon the circle of the earth, and sees the inhabitants as grasshoppers?" That is no other than the Eternal, the eye of all to one.

Like the generation of the desert we cannot enter that Promised Land either because we see too little or because we see too much.

A most beautiful Hassidic story was told by Rabi S. Carlebach about Rebe Levi Itschak of Berdichev and the Alter Rebbe of Lubavitch. For the former there was no world, just one G-d. For the latter, there was one G-d, but yet, there was also the world. They once met on a wedding that they both had to perform. They were on their way to the *huppah*, the wedding canopy, and the door they had to pass was very small. One said to the other: "You go first". The other said: "No, you go first". They argued for a while and finally Rebe Itschak of Berdichev said. "You know what? Let's go through the wall". The Alter Rebbe said: "No let the door become wider!"

For most of the people the door is too small or the walls are too dense. The door is too small for those that are swallowed by routine and patterns. The walls, in the other hand, are too hard for those that will have their illusions and wishful thinking checked by reality. Two groups, however, will still be able to have access: those that can go through the wall and those that can make the door wider. The first group is the one that through their spiritual and intuitive sensibility can soften the divisions, the walls, of this world. The second is the one that is so attuned to the world, to the way reality is presented to us, that they will gradually make the door widen. They have brought us the internet and will bring us so many incredible tools for making our door wider.

The world of the future will be a world of great accesses. People will have to be Rabi Akiba, so as not to get lost in this land, in this place. They will migrate through doors never before imagined. But they must be revolving doors that will as much take you out as bring you back in. Depending on how much they revolve, the era when the Name will be One, will give way to a time when all will be One. Or better, the door will be so wide that there will be no more space for walls.

On that day, ancient prophesies accessed through place, will be fulfilled in time. Their proclamation will echo from end to end of space:

"Tell Jerusalem that the end of exile has arrived...", "Awake, awake, O Jerusalem! Turn, turn, and leave that place!"; "Pass, pass through the gate... G-d made himself heard in all the world: Thy redemption has arrived!"

Isaiah, 40, 51, 54.

*"Open the gate for us, at the time of its closing,
as day is ending.
Day pales and the sun rests at the horizon;
make us enter through Thy gates!"*

Neilah prayer, at the end of Yom Kippur